KNOWING THROUGH POETIC REFLECTION

Brian E. Wakeman

Illustrated by Poems of
Brian E. Wakeman

Pen Press

Scripture quotations taken from
The Holy Bible, New International Version (Anglicised edition)
Copyright © 1979, 1984, 2011 by Biblica
(formerly International Bible Society).
Used by permission of Hodder & Stoughton Publishers,
a Hachette UK company. All rights reserved.
'NIV' is a registered trademark of Biblica
(formerly International Bible Society).
UK trademark number 1448790

Scripture quotations are also from The Holy Bible,
English Standard Version, published by Publishers © 2001 by
Crossway Bibles, a division of Good News Publishers.
Used by permission. All rights reserved.

First published in Great Britain by Pen Press

All paper used in the printing of this book has been made from
wood grown in managed, sustainable forests.

ISBN 978-1-78003-617-5

Printed and bound in the UK
Pen Press is an imprint of
Indepenpress Publishing Limited
25 Eastern Place
Brighton
BN2 1GJ

A catalogue record of this book is available from
the British Library

Cover design by Jacqueline Abromeit

Dedication

To Hazel

"The wings that have helped me fly"

To my grandchildren:

Ella-Marie, Jonathan, Pippa,
Anna-Lisa, Daniel, and Roseanne

"But from everlasting to everlasting
The Lord's love is with those who fear him,
And his righteousness with their
Children's children"
Psalm 103,17

ACKNOWLEDGEMENTS

This book draws on traditions of Christian faith and devotion, and on scholarship that have been passed on to me. Where I have quoted writers for their insights I have made reference to my sources wherever possible.

I am grateful to the Senior Pastor of West Street Baptist Church Dunstable, UK for consent to publish the chapter Art and Poetry. The views expressed are the author's and not necessarily those of the pastors and elders of the church.

I acknowledge the inspiration and help of several poetry web sites quoted in the book, and particularly to the research site CRIAN (Christian Research in Action). (http://transformingresearch.ning.com/).

A big 'thank you' to friends and colleagues, who have read my poems, commented, critiqued, and encouraged my writing. I hope they will recognise the revisions I have made in the light of peer review. Readers are invited to comment on my writing at http://www.surveymonkey.com/s/QBZY9YC

Any errors or mistakes are the author's responsibility, and the views expressed are his alone and not necessarily those of any of the organisations or societies with which he is associated. If he has inadvertently failed to acknowledge sources correctly or copyright material, he will put that right in future digital or written revisions.

The writer hopes that the issues and insights the book raises will be of interest to a wide range of readers with different cultural backgrounds even though he writes from his own cultural background in the UK.

Finally a big 'thank you' to Hazel my wife for her patience and love, for believing in me and in my writing.

CONTENTS

INTRODUCTION

There are several ways of approaching this book:

- Some readers have requested a more permanent copy of the author's poems, so they can read them at their leisure.

- Some readers may encounter the poems for the first time.
  I hope you will make space to reflect on them, that some may delight or amuse, and maybe some may speak to you personally.

- Other readers may be interested in the themes and issues discussed in the commentary on *Knowing through Poetic Reflection*. The author believes he has contributed fresh ideas in each of the chapters.

- Of course, you may wish to read both the poems and the discussions, or just the chapters that interest you.

The book arose out of several requests for a more permanent record for some of the poems the author made available at Art Continuers, Dunstable, UK to stimulate ideas for painting, and thought about Christian beliefs. He has assembled a selection of verses that readers can refer to separately in the chapters, or as part of the discussion. So one audience might be readers who enjoy or value poetry, or who would like a collection of the author's work. They can skip over the commentary and the more theoretical or technical sections.

The title *Knowing through Poetic Reflection* expresses the kernel of what he is trying to say. A reflection is the representation of something in a faithful way, or the showing of an image of something. Many of these poems try to communicate scenes, events or thoughts.

In another sense, reflection is thinking deeply or carefully about something. Writing this book has been a journey for the author in thinking about poetry as a form of communication. This is particularly true of expressing ideas about the Christian Faith, and about poetry as a way of speaking to people.

There is a second audience in mind. Some readers may be interested in the themes of this book. In the reflections, the author hopes to have been able to contribute to a more serious study of the following:

Poetry and Art;

Poetry and Humour, and the Therapeutic Effects of Poetry ;

Poetry and Prophecy;

Poetry as Theological reflection;

Poetry as Wisdom;

The Anatomy of Poetry;

Poetry as a way of Knowing and Research;

Developing the Use of Poetry in the Church.

Research Methodology

A third audience might be scholarly readers in the fields of Mission Studies, Christianity and Art, the nature of poetry, poetry as a therapeutic process, Biblical Studies, Practical Theology, and qualitative research. The author believes he has something of interest to add to each of these disciplines.

'Poetry and Art' describes and illustrates using Art and Poetry as a medium for mission at Art Continuers at The Way, Dunstable, Bedfordshire, UK. The author would be interested to hear of other examples of employing Art and Poetry in evangelism or holistic mission.

He hopes 'Poetry and Humour' makes you smile. It is encouraging to see Christian joy and laughter being respectfully restored in churches. 'A joyful heart is good medicine'.[1] In this chapter, I also illustrate with examples of my verse, poetry as a way of coping with illness, a form of therapy for a cancer patient. Several poems have been appreciated by health professionals, and may be of interest to a wider audience of readers in the medical profession.

'Poetry as Theological Reflection' gives examples of how readers can use verse forms as a means of meditation in personal devotions or meditative 'quiet times'. There are poems as a response to sermons, and some, with more serious thinking and reflection about Christian belief.

In 'Poetry and Prophecy', the writer explores the similarities and differences between the two, and what prophecy may look like in the Church today. He speaks of poems that may have a 'prophetic edge'. He has valued readers' criticism, and appreciative responses to these ideas in earlier drafts.

In the 'Anatomy of Poetry' he explains the form and structure of some of his poems in more detail and a little about the process and circumstances of writing.

'Poetry as Wisdom' explores the nature of wisdom, and some features of Wisdom literature in the Old Testament. He notes how the New Testament writers speak of Wisdom. In this discussion he illustrates aspects of what might be called 'wisdom' that are reflected in some of his poems.

The author hopes that the ideas in 'Poetry and Knowing', and about poetry and research that have been shared with peers, may be of interest to the wider research community in education, and allied professions. The author argues that poetry can be a process and product of research. A recurring theme in these chapters is the relating of faith to life, and professional practice.

The penultimate chapter lays out the importance of Poetry in the Bible, and Church worship. It makes an appeal to restore the use of poetic language and forms in corporate and private lives. Readers are invited to reflect about the practical suggestions that are made.

---

[1] Proverbs 17, 22 (ESV)

Then finally, the author explains the research methodology adopted in preparing the book. The enterprise has been a form of action research into his practice.

So this book is compiled as a contribution to writing on Christianity and the arts, and the place of poetry in the mission and ministry of the church. The author's prayer is that parts of the book or individual poems may also speak to people. It is his hope that the Christian Faith expressed may illuminate, and encourage some readers in their experience of life, and their understanding of the Living God.

Earlier drafts of the book invited reader reaction and feedback on the ideas expressed. Suggestions have been included in this revision. Readers are encouraged to respond or comment on their reading to the author to continue this conversation on poetry at brian.wakeman@OCMS.ac.uk.

CHAPTER 1

ART and POETRY in Mission

Art and poetry can have an important role in Christian mission. We can be unnecessarily suspicious or even dismissive about Art, or about Poetry without realising how significant they are in the story of our Faith.

The Church has had an ambivalent attitude to Art through its history in the West. Art has almost been synonymous with 'Christian Art' in some eras as the classical paintings of Biblical themes illustrate. Paintings, murals, stained glass and carvings in parish churches in the UK fill places of worship with colour and visual symbols that point beyond the works of Art to Christian beliefs. There have also been periods of iconoclasm, rejection of artistic images, and austere unembellished simplicity in some non-conformist traditions.

Poetry too has a positive and rich tradition illustrated in the writing genres of the Church's scriptures, and in hymnology and worship. Poetry has had a powerful impact on the spiritual life of believers through the reading of the literary forms, rhythm and imagery of the Bible, and through singing Psalms, hymns, and songs.

This chapter has two purposes: firstly, it describes an example of Art as Mission. It portrays the activity of the 'Art Continuers' group (Dunstable, UK), and reproduces some of the cards used to inspire painting for members. The chapter makes these more widely available in response to requests for a more permanent collection. Secondly, the chapter describes some of the motivation and thinking behind the convening of the group, the author's reflection about Art, Art and Mission, and the use of poetry for communicating Christian beliefs.

The author hopes the chapter will stimulate readers to think of ways Art and Poetry can be used as tools of mission or evangelism in their culture.

Daffodils at Ascott House.
Watercolour and inks, by the author

ART and POETRY

Several people have asked me to collect together some of the poems I have composed over four years or so, and make them available in a more permanent form. They were written to try to inspire painting at Art Continuers, a group I have helped to coordinate at 'The Way'[1] in Dunstable, UK. The group is a mixture of 'beginners', 'continuers' and accomplished artists in watercolour and other media. Some members have been self-motivated, but others have asked for some inspiration and guidance to 'get them going'. We have offered suggestions of pictures, colour 'ideas sheets', exemplars, some teaching, and lots of encouragement. I have produced small cards to assist this process. These cards have had a small picture of the current topic, some guidance on technique, and often a verse. Here is one on the theme of 'Horses'.

Horses

Photo: the author

(Technique guidance overleaf…)

"As I watched you gallop in the paddock free
Your tails flowing , manes wind-blown in ecstasy,
Chestnuts leading, piebalds , black and white behind
Praise for your designer flooded to my mind.
Shetland ponies, chestnut Suffolks, feathered Shires,
Powerful Clydesdales, Clevelands for the squires;
Thoroughbreds for speed, hunters for the chase,
Draughts and Arabs displaying power or grace;
Horses: similar shapes, but varying height,
So observe 'proportion', 'perspective', and light.
Capture the 'pose', the colours, gloss and sheen.
Plan light and shadow as you design your scene."
BEW '09
West Street Baptist Church *The Way*

---

[1] "The Way" is part of the ministry of West Street Baptist Church, Dunstable, Beds, UK.

1. Using the resources, draw the outline shape or trace the horse from Jean Filler Scott's book 'Painting Animal Friends' (North Light Books, Cincinnati, Ohio, US. 2005. £16.99p)
2. Think about your scene, the foreground, middle, and background.
3. Colours will depend on your horse and the composition
4. Useful colours: raw and burnt sienna; light red; warm sepia; raw and burnt umber; Payne's Grey; indigo; and of course greens
5. Use under-washes; dry-brush technique; fans; fine brushes for horse's coat, mane and tail.
6. You don't have to be too photographic. Capture the essence...

I had researched some background about horses, and techniques of painting. The poem reflects this. There were colour copy reference sheets available for people illustrating various types of horses. Paintings of horses were displayed and discussed. So, you can see how the poem was designed to arouse interest, inform, and give painting tips. The principle underlying the purpose and motivation for organising the group is reflected in the line, 'Praise for your designer flooded to my mind.'

The next card hints how we follow the seasons for ideas in painting. In April, Ascott House[2] near Leighton Buzzard, Bedfordshire, UK has what someone has claimed to be 'the greatest show on Earth' of daffodils. They are simply dazzling. I take photographs of local places and attempt to portray the atmosphere in watercolour and verse.

In this next poem, I have introduced gentle humour, "I know we knock the bankers", and ideas on which I could expand in conversations during the two hours of the Tuesday mornings:

"...contemplate the infinite.
Here you can withdraw and pray"

A small group drove over to Ascott to enjoy the atmosphere and spectacle.

---

[2] http://www.ascottestate.co.uk/ (accessed April 24th, 2012)

Photo: the author

Draw or trace main outline. Then prepare plenty of your colours
1. Wet sky. Use cobalt wash at top and cerulean at the bottom.
2. Blot out the clouds.
3. Paint the house: BU; BS; PG windows
4. Work down picture, inserting trees.
If you are feeling brave, put in some daffs or narcissi.

Art Continuers

For subtleties of colour: cadmium pale,
Late daffs dazzling in the vale,
Trumpets nodding in the breeze,
Clipped hedges, manicured box trees,
Magnificent Magnolia, Camellia in white,
Fox Gloves later, a gardener's delight;
The fountains, Cupid, the Narcissi:
The bewitching perfume of 'Pheasant's Eye'.
Take the A505-A418 near Wing.
It's not too far to travel that's the thing!
Inside the rambling Rothschild's mansion,
I know we knock bankers (It's the fashion),
Are priceless treasures: Reynolds, & Stubbs.
There are places to sit in the quiet
To 'contemplate the Infinite'.
Here you can withdraw and pray.
You'll need an NT card, or have to pay,
And if you need a drink don't even ask.
Make some tea for your Thermos flask!

"Be on your guard against all kinds of greed; a man's life does not consist in the abundance of his possessions" Luke 12,15

West Street Baptist Church *The Way*

The next card shows two demonstration paintings of mine, one copying Karen Simmons' beautiful painting of a bluebell wood, and the other a copy of Karen Chippindale's painting. We draw attention to the work of artists and recommend their works and books.

Author's BW copy of K Simmons

Painting for Pleasure
Art Continuers

1. Sketch or trace the main outline.
2. Colours: Transparent yellow;
Sunlight green; raw sienna, raw
umber, ultra marine violet (try
Alizarin touch) Windsor blue;
Prussian blue; burnt sienna, sepia;
Terry Harrison Greens; shadow;
3. Or try K. Chippindale's wet-into-
wet bluebells.

*"The vivid sweep of blue in an
English woodland... makes one
catch one's breath, and the scent of
the bluebells... the light falls
through the thin Spring foliage and
dapples the bluebells."*
*"Throughout history our creativity
has revealed... our... beliefs"*
Karen Simmons 1995 (2000)
Batsford ISBN 0 7134 9199 4

Painting Flowers

West Street Baptist Church   *The Way*

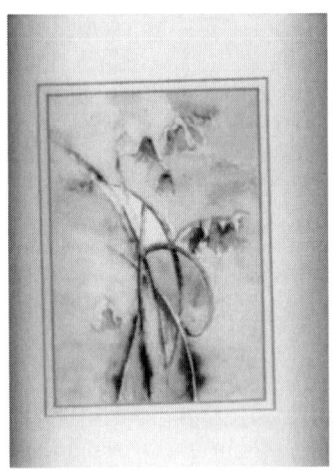

Author's copy of K. Chippindale

18

This is my poem 'Bluebells' that was shared with group:

Bluebells

And there we saw a sea of ethereal blue
Receding mistily from our roadside view.
Beneath the canopy's sunlit green
A carpet of bluebells could be seen
Of a cobalt tint with a violet haze
With tracks and paths and deer bye-ways.
Here and there the morning light
Illuminated a variant bluebell white.
Fallen trees moulded by decay
Reminded of a sculptor at play.
A radiance filled the woodland scene
Exhibiting a study of shades of green.
The perfume moved the dullest heart
Signature of the Creator's art.

This poem tries to capture the scene, appealing to the senses, and evokes memories of readers who have seen the bluebells. It takes joy in the beauty of the wood of late April in Ashridge Forest, but points beyond the scene to the Creator. Karen Simmons captures something of the numinous, spiritual quality.

> "The vivid sweep of blue in an English woodland… makes one catch one's breath, and the scent of the bluebells… the light falls through the thin Spring foliage and dapples the bluebells."
> "Throughout history our creativity has revealed…our… beliefs"[3]

As a teenager, I was deeply moved by the poetry of Gerard Manley Hopkins.[4] Laurann de Verteuil comments:

---

[3] Karen Simmons 1995 (2000) *Painting Flowers*. Batsford
ISBN 0 7134 9199 4
[4] *Selected Poems of Gerard Manley Hopkins*. Ed. Reeve J. 1953.
London: Heinemann Educ. Books

"Hopkins explicitly states his admiration of nature in his journals, writing, "I do not think I have ever seen anything more beautiful than the bluebell I have been looking at. I know the beauty of our Lord by it" (Miller, 313). Hopkins' joy, even euphoria, at re-discovering nature then is because he sees all things as created in Christ. Christopher Devlin points out that "[Hopkins] thinks of Christ's created nature as the original pattern of creation, to a place in which all subsequent created beings must attain in order to be complete" (Miller, 312-3). This evaluation seems justified when we read the following verses: "I walk, I lift up heart, eyes, / Down all that glory in the heavens to glean our Saviour" ('Hurrahing in Harvest', ll. 5-6). Similar to Arnold's belief that God's love can be felt through fellow-feeling, Hopkins maintains through his journals and through his poetry that God remains omnipresent and that one simply has to look, really look at the beauty of nature to see the beauty of Christ [5]

The Art Continuers group has aims that are expressed through the activities organised. The first is to introduce people to watercolours, and to offer further advice on how to develop skills. The second is to provide an atmosphere where people feel welcome, where they are valued, and can appreciate the Christian agape love expressed. We wish to serve our local community, and model God's loving-kindness. The third is to celebrate the beauties of the Creation through Art. Finally and most importantly, we want to introduce people to the Creator, so we take opportunity to talk about Christian beliefs and offer further courses to explore and discuss the Faith. We work at creating an atmosphere and

---

[5]http://www.victorianweb.org/authors/arnold/deverteuil.html (accessed April 24th, 2012) Laurann de Verteuil '07, English Literature 99HL, *Literature 1830–1914*, University of Glasgow, 2007. Reviving God: a study of Matthew Arnold and Gerard Manley Hopkins' religious belief.

ethos of acceptance, and loving-kindness. Our prayer is that members of the Art team will model aspects of God's Kingdom, what society might be like in God's design, and thereby make our words about the Faith more credible.

I have been developing my underlying beliefs and values (a theological perspective) on Art over the several years of working at Art Continuers, through wider reading, and reflection. Briefly, I see Art as one of the aspects or modes of reality in God's creation. It is a form of creative expression, and a distinct realm of human experience.

I have found it interesting to trace artistic endeavour through the Bible (e.g. from Genesis where man is created in the image of God, to the artwork of Bezalel and Oholiab for the Tabernacle[6], and the building and furnishing of Solomon's Temple[7], and re-building in Ezra's time).[8] Then I learned more about Christian religious art down through the centuries.[9] Of course, the Bible forbids the use of art to make images for idolatry. The Church has turned its face away from Art and destroyed icons and carvings at different times. 'The role of the Church to the arts has oscillated between that of patron and persecutor' to use Crum Ewing's apt sentence.[10]

However, for me creativity is one way of expressing 'the image of God'[11] in our human lives. Not only can Art bring great joy, satisfaction and fulfilment, but also we can express ideas, make interpretations, and communicate in visual forms. We can delight in good things (as Paul says, "Whatever is true, what ever is noble, whatever is right, whatever is pure, what ever is lovely, whatever is admirable – if anything is excellent or praiseworthy – think about such things").[12] I believe

---

[6] Exodus 31, 1-11 NIV

[7] I Kings 6 NIV

[8] Ezra 3 NIV

[9] *The Lion Companion to CHRISTIAN ART.* Michelle Brown

[10] Crum Ewing, A.H. *Art and the Christian Church*

[11] Genesis 1,26-28. "Then God said, 'Let us make man in our image, in our likeness, and let them rule…' NIV 1993. Cambridge: Univ. Cambridge.

[12] Philippians 4,8 NIV.

Christians should not turn our backs to Art, but redeem it for God. Yes, we can distinguish between the fallen, distorted, the twisted, and despairing in Art on the one hand, from on the other hand the beautiful, the ennobling, and the celebration of life. We can critique evil and meaningless in society that is reflected in some Art. The Christian can analyse the fallen, the misdirected creativity, and the distortions of goodness in Art. We are called to redeem Art for God.[13] This does not mean an irritating moralising about artists' work, where priests preside and critique artists. Rather it means uncovering God's original intentions for this mode of reality, and expressing God's goodness creatively. We can take delight in being creative, reflecting God's image, and develop appreciation of the artistic skills of others.

This may mean broadening or revising our understanding of the nature and purposes of Art. As D.E.H. Thistlewaite comments:

> "In the last few decades, the public meaning of 'art', that is to say, of living art, has undergone such a transformation that the more culturally conservative Christians among us, looking in the pigeonholes in which we thought to find 'art' would find them empty. The old classifications have gone and some of the old language has flown."[14]

His article is helpful in developing understanding of how Christians can engage with Art. 'We can criticize the new Art for lacking meaning, humanity or intelligibility or beauty...' He asks, 'What is Art like if touched by Christ?' Among the pointers he gives is that Christian Art deals with intelligible

[13] See *Art & Soul* by Hilary Brand & Adrienne Chaplin
[14] 'Art' in *New Dictionary of Christian Apologetics*. See also Geoff Kersey's inspirational book *London in Watercolour*. 2009. Tunbridge Wells: Search Press p.25 that was recommended to the group.

realities. It should serve and bless, and it has something of 'God' about it: wisdom, grace, authority, and beauty.[15]

Certainly, Art Continuers reflects a range of ideas and understandings of Art from the representational, the botanical, to the conceptual and abstract more modern approaches. We employ artistic expression as a medium or channel for exploring and expressing faith.

This next card invites the group members to reflect through the poem and their own painting about Britain's Christian heritage. Painting and poetry can become a celebration of culture, but also a critique of society and increasing secularization.

Geoff Kersey: London in Watercolour. Search Press

Colours:
1. Wet sky. Use cobalt wash at top and cerulean at the bottom.
2. Experiment with Palace stone: Naples Yellow and pink or raw sienna. Notice the shadows.
3. Statue Raw Sienna + burnt umber

Art Continuers

Buckingham Palace

Seat of our Monarchy
Steeped in our history,
Central to our Constitution
The Nations' evolution:
Parliamentary democracy,
Avoiding evils of autocracy.

Our 'moral reservoir' is running dry.
Leaders need to stop and ask, 'Why?'
Return to the Code of truthfulness
Love of neighbour and faithfulness.
We need to 'renew in our mind',
Ideas of service of a 'Queenly' kind.

So as we paint the Royal Palace,
Showing respect for 'Sovereign Grace',
Getting a right proportion and perspective,
Spend time to be a little reflective.
Draw on our Christian heritage streams
To renew moral vision and spiritual dreams.

West Street Baptist Church   *The Way*

---

[15] See also Rookmaaker H.R. 1970 *Modern Art and The Death of Culture*. Leicester: IVP. Seerveld C. 1980. *Rainbows for The Fallen World*. Toronto. *Art & The Soul. Signposts for Christians in The Arts*. Brand H. & Chaplin A. 1999. Carlisle: Piquant. *Imagine A vision for Christians in The Arts*. Turner S. 2001. Downers Grove, US: IVP

Our hope is that group members may be given insight into the power and relevance of Christianity through the painting, and in reflection about the ideas in the poem, and by discussion during the morning. Painting and poetry are invitational as well as expressive.

There appears to be a healing power in Art for some people.[16] Art therapists have a much deeper understanding of this.[17] Painting can have therapeutic power. Members of our group used the words, 'absorbing', 'relaxing', 'immersing oneself', 'members are so funny', 'like-minded people', 'encouragement'. Painting not only gives them an interest that takes them out of the house, avoiding downward spirals of negative depressive thinking, but also stimulates imagination and fulfilling creativity.

Painting has taught me more focused observation, how to pay more attention to appreciate the natural world and human situations. This point is reinforced in discussions in the group. Several comments in an Art Continuers' Feed Back Survey

---

[16] See stories of e.g. Graham Hudson

http://www.eauk.org/culture/forum-for-change/culture-footprint/index.cfm?page_no=1#articles

[17] Ed. Dalley T. 1984. *Art as Therapy: An Introduction to the Use of Art as a Therapeutic Technique.* London: Routledge

The Publisher's statement: '*Art as Therapy* introduces the theory and practice of art therapy in a concise, accessible and informative way. Tessa Dalley's introduction gives an overview of basic issues, research and development. Subsequent chapters, written by specialists, are chosen to demonstrate the ways in which art therapy can be applied to different client groups, in a variety of clinical settings. These include children, adolescents suffering from anorexia nervosa, the mentally handicapped, the elderly and terminally ill, those in psychiatric hospitals and prison inmates. Illustrated case studies provide visual explanations for the art therapy processes and the final chapter discusses training for the profession. *Art as Therapy* has been welcomed by art therapists, social workers, psychologists, nurses and teachers'.

express their pleasure and fulfilment[18], and appreciate the human fellowship the art group brings. I have noticed that painting has attracted people who are hurting. We have had several recently bereaved people come to the group, and cancer or ex-cancer patients. Painting provides an absorbing 'distraction', which is a key feature of pain management.[19]

'Where does the poetry fit-in?" you might ask. As I have tried to illustrate earlier, poems perform several roles. They stimulate interest, and inform and give tips for painting. We hope one artistic creative medium will inspire another: poetry and painting. They are a vehicle for communication. The poems are also designed to arouse interest in the Christian Faith. They introduce elements of spiritual experience using the imagery, emotional impact, and the oblique quality of verse. We pray the words may 'speak' to someone personally about 'faith' issues. We hope the Holy Spirit will work through the medium of poetry.

We have been asked if only Baptists or believers can come and paint. I have explained that the group is open to all we can fit-in.[20] The Church wishes to serve the people in the local community. Similarly some might question whether it is only 'Christian Art' we encourage. It is appropriate now to address

---

[18] Spring 2009. Out of 23 respondents (out of group of 30) twenty people commented on aspects of fellowship in a Feedback: "The things I enjoy about coming to Art Continuers are…"
Ten people mentioned 'pleasure', 'learning', 'interest',
Five mentioned the 'atmosphere'
[19] http://pain.about.com/od/livingwithchronicpain/a/distraction_from_pain.htm (accessed 8/5/2011)
http://www.backcare.org.uk/779-5725/Dealing-with-back-pain-flare-ups.html (accessed 8/5/2011)
Shone N.1992 *Coping Successfully With Pain*. London: Sheldon Press. SPCK
Wells C.& Nown G.1996. *The Pain Relief Handbook*, London: Vermillion. Ebury Press
[20] Mid 30s in January 2013.

the question further: 'What do people mean by *'Christian Art'*?[21]

"Christian" Art as a noun is probably best seen as an umbrella term for art through the ages with Christian topics or focus such as those artists and works in the Lion Companion.[22] 'Christian' Art as an adjective can refer to the Christian philosophical assumptions or world-views that the artist brings to their work: understanding of the nature of reality; beliefs about God, truth, the 'good life' and aesthetics.

Is there such a thing as Christian Art, any more that 'Christian Geography' or Maths, or Science? Some say, 'No, Science is Science, and Art is plain Art'. There are artists who happen to be Christians, but that does not necessarily mean their Art is 'Christian'. There are societies for Christian artists[23] as a web search will reveal, who may or may not work on theological themes. Some societies make it an aim to 'be salt and light' in the Art world. It is interesting to read the web pages of the organisations for statements of 'purposes'.

For hundreds of years Art was almost synonymous with 'Christian' Art. The great artists expressed Biblical and religious themes.[24] Art was sponsored by the Church in medieval times. Art decorates churches, expressing the faith visually in carvings, banners, murals, and stained glass. English cathedrals are sacred art galleries full of visual expressions of faith to the glory of God. Works depict Bible stories, symbols, icons, transmitting the faith to the congregation. Before printing, the Parish church with its architecture, furnishing

---

[21] See 'What is Christian Art?' in *Christian Art* by Michelle P. Brown
[22] *Christian Art* by Michelle Brown
[23] www.christianartists-network.org/page/uk/76/Aboutus.html (accessed 14 May 2011)
www.facebook.com/group.php?gid=41827304608 (accessed 14 May 2011)
http://www.s-i-a-c.org/english/index.htm (accessed 14 May 2011)
[24] See e.g. Dorment R. 2011 Art With A Touch of Heaven. *Daily Telegraph* article July 5th, 2011 about Exhibitions: 'Devotion By Design' at the National Gallery, and 'Treasures From Heaven' at the British Museum'.

and decoration was a visual book: wall paintings of Bible stories, beam-ends carved with heroes and villains, brasses and tombs for the rich and powerful longing for everlasting life. However, the works of Art were not necessarily produced by 'good' Christians. Dedicated monks made wonderful illuminated manuscripts, but the church sponsored secular artists too.

Much of 'church' Art is a medium for expressing religious stories, Christian ideas and symbols. Some Christians have destroyed art as 'unreformed' or idolatrous as in some responses in Puritan times. Today visual expressions may be discouraged in some Christian denominations (e.g. some Strict Brethren Halls). Other Christians limit or confine Art to mission or evangelism. In this sense 'Christian Art' is graphic design for book covers, for tracts, and paintings for Sunday school illustrations of Bible stories. This restricted view of the place of Art in church life avoids charges of making idolatrous images, but is partially blind to the creative gifts of God in Scripture and to the talents of believers. They miss art as rejoicing in the Creation, and as a way of exploring and expressing our shared human experience. Art can be a means of expressing and communicating aspects of the human condition. Artists can paint inspired by their faith, or as a visual means of expressing faith. Christians bring their world-view to their art as we discussed earlier.

In our group, painting has value intrinsically as a dimension of created reality. It is a way of expressing our creativity. It has a social dimension, creating opportunity for friendship and fellowship. Painting can bring healing for the soul. It is a visual medium together with written poetry, pictures in language, for arousing faith, and interest in Christianity. Art can be a channel for God's Holy Spirit to work in people's lives. All these dimensions can be in place: the atmosphere, the expressive and visual aspect of Art, the stimulus and message of poetry, but if the Spirit of God is not present then there are vehicles, but no fuel for power. There are sails, but with no breeze, there is no power, no direction or impact.

One of our group members showed me her painting of windmills. She asked what I noticed, and explained that some of the mill sails were chained and powerless. This next poem develops these ideas:

Windmills in Autumn

The sails are motionless
Without the wind blowing.
Machinery is powerless
Without energy flowing.
Our power potential
Is not existential
Without the Spirit
God's pneuma' in it.

Lord, help us to invite
Your transforming light.
We need faith to receive
To more fully believe
This season of Advent
Why Christ was sent.

In this next poem, I had been reflecting about yachts and the power of the wind. Wind is an analogy, a metaphor of the 'pneuma', the energy of the Spirit in the New Testament.

Photo: Wikipedia

I've experimented painting 'Spinnakers' in water colour and gouache this week.
We'll talk about the techniques and the colours.
Beware of breaking copyright if you sell a painting.

'Pneuma' , Summer 2010

I couldn't sleep that night,
So I arose from the darkness of the night
And painted yachts 'all at sea',
Blown along, spinnakers free.
Alone, becalmed and static,
But with wind-filled sails emphatic
Power, racing up the Solent!
I paused to reflect a moment,
Praying to feel the exhilaration
Of God's Spirit's inspiration.
We so often forget or fail
To unfurl our faith the spiritual sail.
"In our union with Christ,
He has blessed us with every spiritual
blessing..." Ephesians 1,3.

The reader can see how we try to communicate Christian truth through the poem. My prayer was that group members may sense 'the breeze' and respond. It is my hope that while painting we may feel the Spirit of God speaking to our minds and emotions.

'Doorways and Windows' made a productive theme in our painting. When I was visiting Winchcombe, an old Cotswold town in Gloucestershire, I took a photograph of steps leading up to a door. They became a symbol for our central purpose for the Art group: in setting-up opportunities to express artistic themes we provide steps up to the door of the Christian faith. I have a longing for people to use the steps provided and to enter the door.[25] There is also the idea of the door as a symbol of death, and entering eternal life.

Who Can Tell Us?

Just a step or two
Up to the door
And then we're through:
And what's more
It's warmer inside
Than the chill outside.
But what's it really
Like, the 'inside' view?
I suppose ideally
We'll know too
From One who's been
Through the door
Who's clearly seen
And can tell us more…

Cotswold House
Winchcombe, Gloucestershire
Photo: The author

---

[25] John 10,9. A.V. "I am the door".

More recently we have used poems to stimulate painting about the season: 'Amazing Blooms in Mexico'; 'The Priory'; 'The Canal at Marsworth'; 'Pumpkins at this time of the Year'; 'Windmills in Autumn'; and 'Downton Abbey'.

I found an amazing set of coloured illustrations of varieties of Dahlias in a gardening magazine[26] which we used to inspire our painting. This poem 'Late Summer' provided interest and discussion about Dahlias in our gardens:

Late Summer

Amazing blooms in Mexico
Were discovered by Francisco
Hernandez in 1615
When Aztec decorations were seen.
Amazing blooms brought back to Spain
And on to Holland again
From where our species came.
Dahlias from Dahl's name:
Coccinea, Barkeriae
Dissecta, Cuspidata!
Food for butterflies
And earwigs we despise!
The tubers go into dormancy
If they are kept 'frost free',
To bloom again
Symbol of the resurrection!

Several members of the group worked on the textures of the stone gateway of Dunstable Priory, Bedfordshire, UK, that I had photographed. They practised making 'greens' for the foliage seen through the gate.

---

[26] Gardeners' World.
http://www.gardenersworld.com/galleries/album.aspx?albumId=8
(accessed Sept. 4th, 2012)

The Priory, Dunstable

The Priory House view
Buttressed against the clouds and sky blue,
The tower stands strong and timeless.
There's a haven of peace from High Street stress.
Mottled Totternhoe stone of a sun-lit hue:
Medieval arches, stone masons' arcades.
The Gateway welcomes, persuades
Of faith for our generation, secular youth,
To endure hardship and to search for truth.
We imagine monastic life now grassed unseen,
And reflect on where Queen Eleanor has been.
There's a restored ancient garden
Reminding of healing and pardon.
There's a kind of reservoir of grace
We need to preserve in this place.

I provide accompanying coloured pictures for these verses, often from my photographs. My wife and I had watched various boats and barges struggle through the shallower late summer water of the Grand Union Canal in Marsworth, UK. Then a pleasure boat taking passengers along the canal grounded, reversed, and just managed to scrape through the shallow water beyond a bridge. This became the inspiration for this next poem:

The Canal, Marsworth

The water was so low
The boats nearly grounded!

This spoke to me of the flowing
Of values on which we are founded,
Draining away without us knowing,
To the 'Brokenness of Britain'
That worries the politician.
Do we need to refresh the streams
Of Christ, and prophets' dreams,
To revive the ancient Hebrew Law

Build bridges to the powerless more,
Follow the old Golden Rule,
Refill the canal's reservoir pool?

My poem Downton Abbey was written in the Autumn, before the ITV Christmas episode 2011 was transmitted that resolved Lady Mary's future.

Downton Abbey[27]

Many folks will be agreeing
That Downton is compulsory viewing.
Society changes with the War.
Matthew enlists, and what is more
The Nation's tense, on tip-toe,
We're all desperate to know
The fate of Lady Mary
(Not of Isabel Crawley).
Tom woos above his class.
Will the Dowager be aghast?
Bates returns with clear intention.
Carson craves for old distinction.
Human frailty we all conceal
Downton Abbey will reveal.
Footman, maid, Earl or Count:
All must give an account.

As we painted, there was much animated discussion about incidents and relationships depicted in the series. It was interesting how much attention the series captivated in the press and in viewing figures.

Autumn provides such rich colours for the artist: siennas, ochres, gold, reds, and browns. Some members of the group tried painting a scene of pumpkins with a cartwheel in the background. We were challenged with ellipsis, spheres and shadows to indicate depth to the picture.

---

[27] See http://www.itv.com/downtonabbey/
(accessed October 4th, 2012)

Autumn

Pumpkins at this time of the year
Fill some children with fun and fear,
(Adults with some soup or pie),
But few pause to ask 'why?'
We celebrate Autumn at all.
Mischief is part of the Fall.
Dark powers yield to the Light:
This the Christian insight.
The orange and gold colouring
Is worth patient painting.
A festival of thanksgiving
In the autumn of living
For the good things we enjoy
Not treats or tricks than can destroy.

At the beginning of a new term we 'loosened-up' as painters
after a long break by painting birds and ducks. A pastor spoke
on the beauty of colour God created.

Mandarin

What a splendid sight,
Almost Oriental,
Dazzling ducks
Dressed up like
Canal boats with
Tassels and stripes
Not castles and roses!
Blues and browns,
Hooker's green
And alizarin,
Magnificent tail
And teasing tresses!
All in praise of his maker!

In this final poem, the author focuses on the negative aspects and effects of being agnostic or atheist. The motivation for writing was to challenge thinking and to break through disinterest or lack of commitment:

Without God

Without God
We're merely molecules,
Chemicals, only material.
Without God
A short breath, then death.
Without God
No morality of any certainty.
Without God
No Incarnation or Resurrection.

Thank God
For His reality:
Eternal life for you and me!

In this chapter, I have illustrated how we use poems at Art Continuers to inspire painting and to communicate ideas about the Christian faith. The purposes of the Art group have been described, and I have discussed what we might mean by 'Christian Art', or a Christian perspective on Art. The picture of the Cotswold cottage steps is a symbol for our work: an invitation to ascend, knock on the door, and enter the Christian faith. I concluded with further examples of poems that some members of the group appreciated and would like to see in a more permanent book form.

The author hopes this chapter provides not only a more permanent record of the poems used in the group, but that it will also contribute to the literature about mission through Art and Poetry, the ministry of creative activity. The author invites readers to share any experiences they have had, or read about, in using Poetry and Art in evangelism or mission.[28] It would be particularly interesting to share experiences from different cultures.[29]

---

[28] Christian Research in Action

http://transformingresearch.ning.com/ (accessed October 4th, 2012)

[29] See http://artculture.com/ (accessed October 4th, 2012)

http://www.africaguide.com/culture/artcraft.htm (accessed October 4th, 2012).

http://www.christianity.com/christian-life/christianity-com-how-should-christians-relate-to-the-arts-shai-linne.html (accessed October 4th, 2012.

http://uk.search.yahoo.com/search?p=Christian Poetry&fr=mcsaoff (accessed October 4th, 2012).

References

Brand H. & Chaplin A. 1999 *Art & The Soul. Signposts for Christians in The Arts*. Carlisle: Piquant.

Brown M.P. 2008. *The Lion Companion to CHRISTIAN ART*. Oxford: Lion Hudson

Crum Ewing, A.H. 1995. Art and the Christian Church. In *New Dictionary of Ethics and Pastoral Theology*. Ed. Atkinson D.J., & Field D.H. 1995. Leicester: IVP.

Chippindale K. http://www.ask4art.com/

Ed. Dalley T. 1984. *Art as Therapy: An Introduction to the Use of Art as a Therapeutic Technique*. London: Routledge

de Verteuil L. '07, English Literature 99HL, *Literature 1830– 1914*, University of Glasgow, 2007. Reviving God: a study of Matthew Arnold and Gerard Manley Hopkins' religious belief.

Dorment R. 2011 'Art With A Touch of Heaven'. *Daily Telegraph* article July 5th, 2011 about Exhibitions: Devotion By Design at the National Gallery, and Treasures From Heaven at the British Museum.

http://www.victorianweb.org/authors/arnold/deverteuil. html (accessed 10/5/2011)

http://pain.about.com/od/livingwithchronicpain/a/ distraction_from_pain.htm (accessed 8/5/2011)

http://www.backcare.org.uk/779-5725/Dealing-with-back- pain-flare-ups.html (accessed 8/5/2011)

http://www.s-i-a-c.org/english/index.htm (accessed 14 May 2011)

Kersey: G. *London in Watercolour*. Tunbridge Wells, Kent: Search Press

Reeve J. Ed. 1953 *Selected Poems of Gerard Manley Hopkins*. London: Heinemann Educ. Books

Scott J.F. 2005. *Painting Animal Friends*, Cincinnati, Ohio, US: North Light Books.

Rookmaaker H.R. 1970 *Modern Art and The Death of Culture*. Leicester: IVP.

Shone N.1992 *Coping Successfully With Pain*. London: Sheldon Press. SPCK

Seerveld C. 1980. *Rainbows for The Fallen World*. Toronto.

Simmons K. 1995 (2000). *Painting Flowers*. London: Batsford.

The Bible. NIV 1993. Cambridge: Univ. Cambridge

Thistlewaite D.E.H 2006 'Art' in *New Dictionary of Christian Apologetics*. Eds. Campbell-Jack & McGrath G.J. 2006. Leicester: IVP

Turner S. 2001 *Imagine: A vision for Christians in The Arts*. Turner S. Downers Grove, US: IVP

Wells C.& Nown G.1996. *The Pain Relief Handbook*. London: Vermillion. Ebury Press

www.christianartists-network.org/page/uk/76/Aboutus.html (accessed 14 May 2011)

www.ascottestate.co.uk/

Questions for Reflection:

1.   What takes place at ART CONTINUERS?

2.   What were the purposes or aims of the group?

3.   What is Christian Art according to the writer? How far would you agree with his understanding?

4.   How does the poetry fit-in with Art in the narrative?

5.   How is the Christian Faith communicated in the group?

6.   Why did the 'steps and door' become a symbol for the work?

7.   Having followed the writer's descriptions and discussion, what place and potential do Art and Poetry have for Christian service and proclamation in your culture?

CHAPTER 2

POETRY and HUMOUR

This watercolour was for demonstration purposes
at Art Continuers by the author.
The idea was inspired by a trip to Whipsnade Zoo,
and from David Webb's *Animal Painting Workbook* 2007,
Cincinnati, US: David & Charles.

POETRY and HUMOUR

In this chapter, I explore my understanding of humour in poetry. I discuss the positive effects of humour generally, how it can lift our spirits, and be a 'good tonic'. I hope some of these poems prompt a smile, and lift the spirits of readers. Some were written to communicate ideas in a light-hearted way, and others to speak more obliquely through laughter.

Humour in poems can circumnavigate our defences to ideas put more directly, and stimulate thought which can be resisted when received more confrontationally. Humour can be like a 'back door' to the reader's mind. Although this chapter is socially set in the UK, the author hopes that any reader may be able to relate to the use of humour in poetry as a therapeutic process to their own cultural context. How is humour used in your culture as a means of coping with trauma? How could verse be therapeutic in your community?

Firstly, in this chapter, the use of humour in poetry is illustrated with some rhymes for my grandchildren. They were written for fun, just to make them smile. Then I discuss the writing of gentle humorous verse as a means of coping with anxiety and pain in cancer treatment as a kind of 'poetic therapy'. Thirdly there are examples of poems demonstrating a gentle wit. Finally there are examples of sharper lampooning or satire of various social situations. These are not examples of sarcasm as one reviewer suggested, but designed to goad[1] reactions, and unveil our human foolishness.

---

[1] See Ecclesiastes 12,11.

Both my sons, in travel to the Himalayas, and to Uganda have commented separately on the smiles of people they met, of radiance even in poverty. I love to see my grandchildren smiling and try to notice what makes them laugh and giggle. Our spirits are lifted by their infectious laughing. Similarly, the good natured banter and laughter that ripples around our art group (which was discussed in the first chapter) lifts the atmosphere and creates good cheer. Good humour can help me relax, and relieves stress. It can increase a sense of well-being.

When I was a teenager I used to hunt in the doctor's surgery, and the barbers (now promoted to 'men's hairdressers') for a back copy of *The Readers Digest*, first to read "Laughter is the Best Medicine', then "It pays To Increase Your Word Power".[2] Smiles filled-in the waiting time, and distracted the mind.

Melinda Smith, Gina Kemp, and Jeanne Segal, write:[3]

"Humor is infectious. The sound of roaring laughter is far more contagious than any cough, sniffle, or sneeze. When laughter is shared, it binds people together and increases happiness and intimacy. In addition to the domino effect of joy and amusement, laughter also triggers healthy physical changes in the body. Humor and laughter strengthen your immune system, boost your energy, diminish pain, and protect you from the damaging effects of stress. Best of all, this priceless medicine is fun, free, and easy to use".

They summarise 'Laughter as the Best Medicine':

---

[2] http://www.rd.com/   (accessed 17/5/2011)

[3] http://www.helpguide.org/life/humor_laughter_health.htm (accessed 17/5/2011)

http://www.sciencedaily.com/releases/2008/01/080124200913.htm   (accessed 17/5/2011)

"It relaxes the whole body. It relieves physical tension and stress, leaving your muscles relaxed for up to 45 minutes later. Laughter boosts the immune system. ...decreases stress hormones and increases immune cells and infection-fighting antibodies, thus improving your resistance to disease. Laughter triggers the release of endorphins, the body's natural feel-good chemicals. Endorphins promote an overall sense of well-being and can even temporarily relieve pain. Laughter protects the heart. ...improves the function of blood vessels and increases blood flow which can help protect you against a heart attack and other cardiovascular problems."

The ancient writer of the Proverbs knew this too:

"A cheerful heart is good medicine,
But a crushed spirit dries up the bones"

Proverbs 17,22 NIV[4]

Byron Pulsifer echoes my thoughts when he said. "Laughter is one of the best medicines around for relieving stress and for creating a more healthy spirit. And, one of the greatest aspects is that it is totally free and can be done by anyone."[5]

Red Skelton said:

"I live by this credo: Have a little laugh at life and look around you for happiness instead of sadness. Laughter has always brought me out of unhappy situations. Even in your darkest moment, you usually can find something to laugh about if you try hard enough."[6]

---

[4] See for further Biblical quotes on humour and laughter: http://www.openbible.info/topics/humor_and_laughter (accessed 18/5/2011)

[5] http://www.inspirationalquotes4u.com/aboutlaughter/index.html   (accessed 18/5/2011)

[6] http://www.great-inspirational-quotes.com/smile-and-laughter-quotes.html   (accessed 18/5/2011)

I develop this theme later, about laughing at one's self, or situation, as a way of coping with hospital treatment, as a kind of poetic therapy.

Humour in poetry brings to mind the so-called nonsense verses of Edward Lear[7], wacky humour of Spike Milligan[8], that made me smile as a child, and the amusing rhymes of Pam Ayres[9] that made my children smile. More recently, my grandchildren chuckle at Giles Andreas' verses (superbly illustrated by Guy Parker-Rees) in e.g. *Giraffes Can't Dance*.[10]

They are now reading them for themselves, but know them by heart, and will catch me out if I miss a word, or try a short-cut on a page near sleep-time!

Here is my attempt to make them smile after a visit to the zoo at Whipsnade, UK. The giraffes seemed enormous compared to a five-year and little three-year-old:

Mr Giraffe

Are you having a laugh?
Is your neck ten feet long
Cos your feet really pong?

Is it true you're sixteen feet tall,
And you sleep one hour, if at all?
Can you kill a lion with just one kick,
Have six feet tall babies,
Or is that just a trick?

---

[7] See http://www.edward-lear.com/Shop.htm
http://www.pocts.org/poct.php/prmPID/140
(accessed October 4th, 2012)
[8] See http://www.spikemilligan.co.uk/spike-milligan-quotes.html   (accessed October 4th, 2012)
[9] See 'O I wish I'd looked after me teeth'
http://www.pamayres.com/index.php/category/poems/
(accessed October 4th, 2012)
[10] see also *Rumble in The Jungle*, *Commotion in The Ocean* & *The Lion Who Wanted Love*. Orchard Books.

Here is another verse written to make the children smile:

Mr Pussy Cat
Why have you got such long whiskers?
Are they there to tickle your sisters?
And why do you seem to sleep in the day
When we go out to run and to play?
Your warm coat: we want to know how
You take it off without a MEOW!

The reaction from a chuckling five-year-old was: "Grandpa, you're silly!"

This next poem was written for a little girl who was temporarily unhappy about going to primary school:

As I was going to school one day
I saw a teacher going the other way.
She wanted to stay at home and play
Because the children had too much to say!

I wrote a poem after visiting my grandchildren who were full of questions, such as "Yes... but why?" "Grandpa, why...?"

Grandpa, "Why?"
(A rhyme for the girls and Dad to think about!)

'Why can we bounce on the trampoline
But not on 'play dough' or plasticine,
And why does Daddy have a hairy chest
While Mummy wears a pretty vest?
What makes the weeds in the garden grow,
But not some seeds that we try to sow?
Why do ducks flap their wings when they fly?
I'm just inquisitive, and want to know 'why?'

The child's constant questioning can be wearisome as they come to terms with the wider world, seek to understand, and make sense of things. Their inquisitiveness disguises deeper questions that lead to knowledge about the properties of materials, differences in sexes, how things grow, and the physics of flight.

Of course, jokes and laughter can distract us from thinking seriously. They can conceal or cover-over other feelings, pain, deeper worries, or emotional trauma too.

"Even in laughter the heart may ache, and joy may end in grief"

Proverbs 14,3 NIV.[11]

"Laughter cannot mask a heavy heart. When the laughter ends, the grief remains."

Proverbs 14,3, *The Living Bible.*[12]

I remember people laughing at a funeral when some boisterous lads almost stumbled into the open grave. Even in sadness we could laugh, but the heart still ached in bereavement. We can laugh with our mouth but not with the eyes. During a tiring 'best man' long speech at a wedding, I remember laughing because it was expected. This was more of a polite or 'hollow' laugh.

Laughing can exclude those who are not 'in' on the joke. You can feel very uncomfortable when you do not know why people are laughing. Humour and laughter can be directed at people, to mock, or to ridicule. I have had to deal with teenagers in classrooms who have used smirks, laughs and misdirected humour in hurtful and cruel ways, picking on perceived weaknesses or differences. I have observed the sharp humour and sarcasm of teachers to be damaging to fragile self-esteem and confidence.

As a society, are we strangely reluctant to constrain the freedom of expression of humour by comedians? (as the controversy about the Russell Brand affair

---

[11] *Holy Bible. The New International Version*, 1979, Cambridge: C.U.P.
[12] *The Living Bible* 1974. London: Coverdale House Pub.

illustrated). Sir Michael Lyons eventually issued this statement on behalf of the BBC Trust.

> "The BBC Trust represents licence fee payers and on their behalf has a responsibility to safeguard high standards of BBC broadcasts. The Trust is dismayed both that the offensive comments broadcast on the Russell Brand Show on 18 October fell so far short of audiences' legitimate expectations, and by the deplorable intrusion in to the privacy of Mr Sachs and his granddaughter. The transmission of these comments via a BBC Radio programme represents an abuse of the privilege given to the BBC to broadcast to its audiences. On behalf of the BBC, the Trust offers a full and unreserved apology to Andrew Sachs, Georgina Baillie and the rest of his family. The Trust extends this apology to licence fee payers as a whole."[13]

In schools in England, we accept much clearer ethical constraints on humour. We lay down rules and teach principles for respect for other people, and for protecting pupils and teachers from hurtful jibes, bullying through jokes, and cyber bulling 'for a laugh'.

Are there any ethical constraints for the comedian or for humour in poetry?

It seems to me that for Christians there is help in Paul's writings.[14] He says:

> "rid yourselves of… anger, malice, slander… clothe yourself with compassion, kindness, humility, patience… and over all these virtues put on love".

Avoiding anger, malice and slander in humour seem to me to be a very wise set of principles. Kindness, humility and agape love are excellent virtues and motivation for the writer expressing truth.

---

[13] http: //www.bbc.co.uk/bbctrust/news/press_releases /2008/october/russell_brand_show.shtml
[14] Colossians 3,5-17

So what is the role of humour, and laughter, irony, lampooning, or satire in poetry?

I wrote 'The Capable Woman' to make friends smile. I had been reading about the model American woman, and Anglicised the setting:

The Capable Woman. Proverbs 31

(Written tongue in cheek after reading Peter Moore's book,[15] in which he quotes the columnist Ellen Goodman,[16] describing the model American woman.)

> She gets up at 6.00 in the morning
> Jogs before light is dawning.
> After no more than five miles
> She showers, and greets with smiles
> Her husband with breakfast in bed.
> By 7.30 her three children are fed.
> By 8.30, she's rushed the school run.
> Now her life has really begun.
> Kissing her husband goodbye
> She to her office must fly
> To her definitely demanding job:
> So fulfilling to earn a few bob.
> With men she'll be competing
> Attending her million-pound meeting.
> Arriving home harassed and late
> She microwaves food on a plate.
> Then after kids' homework is complete
> They have 'quality time' as a treat.
> Then jaded, at her most alluring
> Her love life is just 'enduring'.
> And oh, by the way, just to say
> She forgot her quiet time today!

---

[15] Peter Moore's book *Disarming The Secular Gods* 1989, Leicester, UK: IVP

[16] See http://www.postwritersgroup.com/goodman.htm (accessed 5 July 2011)

The poem uses gentle humour, exaggeration, and makes light of the notion of 'quality time', jaded lovemaking, and the impossible demands and juggling of priorities that some women have. It concludes with the humorous aside about religious devotions that get squeezed out by a hectic life-style. I hoped some readers might identify with points I made, or at least smile. It was written from an empathetic rather than critical perspective. I have had different responses to The Capable Woman, from amusement, "Ha, ha, ha, I won't show my husband", to offended feelings expressing that I was 'getting at women'. One correspondent thought I was being chauvinistic.

This next poem is a light verse about flying to Geneva from Luton Airport. It captures the experiences, and on re-reading the poem, memories come flooding back for the writer. The process of writing helped the author to cope with some of the anxieties and frustrations of air travel.

Luton To Geneva: New Year's Day 2010

'Checking-in will be quiet today',
Or, so we thought on New Year's Day!
Stop-start, six lines queuing,
Strict security checks ensuing.
Clickety-clack of roller cases,
Lots of seats and empty spaces.
French accents and Polish voices,
Sales in shops, so lots of choices!
Flight delayed so an anxious wait.
Hooray we're off, though somewhat late.
A steep climb with engines' roar;
Soon at 30,000 feet or more.
White clouds below, clear and bright;
The horizon dips as we turn in flight.
Over the Thames, then the Channel coast.
Panini's for sale, or drinks to toast
"To the profits of Easyjet"

Perfumes, and toys, or a necklace set.
Paris in miniature far, far below,
Then the long descent to La Suisse.
(+10 in Geneva, so won't need that fleece).
Down through alpine clouds, along the Lake;
A bumpy landing. Hope the captain's awake!

Writing in a humorous way about experiences of medical treatment for bladder cancer and a blood disorder has helped me cope and lifted spirits. One reaction to being told you have cancer can be to shut down communication and withdraw into yourself. However, writing can help fill the long and anxious hours in waiting rooms, or the empty space lying in hospital beds. It seems to have healing properties, helping me to come to terms and process distressing experience.

Max Pemberton wrote about the dark humour of doctors in 'Doctors Must Laugh in the Face of Death'.[17] He refers to Kate Watson's examination of doctors' use of gallows humour. Pemberton agrees that it can, not only be ethical, but beneficial too. He says:

> From my experience, its function is never to humiliate or belittle patients, but always to help clinicians get on with their jobs. It's not easy to see the frailty of the human condition unravel in front of you… It was the psychoanalyst Sigmund Freud who first catalogued the use of humour as a defence mechanism. He described it as a vital psychological strategy for protecting oneself from the harshness of life. Psychologists now consider it a 'mature' state of emotional development, enabling people to reframe and take control of situations that would otherwise hinder normal functioning.

---

[17] *The Daily Telegraph*, UK. September 29th, 2011

Pemberton says using humour is a way of confronting feelings or thoughts that are otherwise too awful or terrible to talk about.

In this next poem, I make light of a frightening experience with a hospital acquired e-coli infection. I saw a notice on the hospital wall about avoiding spreading infections, and picked up the irony of my position. Gently I point out the contradictions in nursing practice about hygiene, a consultant's detached and brisk visit to the ward, and my anxiety about a heart arrhythmia. I make light of the night noise on the ward, and slow response to an emergency call. I understand the hospital has made use of the poem for training purposes.

"Just One Minute"...

"Patients should avoid spreading infections
By using soap and alcoholic concoctions."
But nurses have clean hands
As everybody understands!
"Lie down dear, you can keep your shoes on.
No risk here of a nasty infection!"
The medical staff from A&E
Were personable, showing us sympathy,
And the consultant displayed precision
In making the treatment decision.

The Acute Care ward was hot, full of cacophonous
    sound,
The only breeze came from a consultant's round.
They wired me up like a robot,
The tabs slipping off, thus losing the plot,
Sending the ECG into toxic spasm
Like a mechanical multiple org - - - -.
'Sleep' at night was a joke, a misnomer.
Loud voices and bleeps will save you from coma.
I didn't use the emergency call. When I used it before
It took seven minutes to respond, so I'm sorry
I've just leaked on the floor!

In 'Reception at Haematology', I use gentle humour to chide the reception I received by a clerk, in contrast with the kindness, and social skill of the doctor herself which allayed anxiety and was healing in itself. The procedure and manner in which patients are greeted, received, processed and treated can add stress, or make them feel so much better.

Reception at Haematology

"Have you got a letter?
An appointment card would be better?"
"Has your name changed, or address?"
(A distancing process, none-the-less).
Passed like a parcel along the line:
"Sit down Sir. There will be fine".
The worry of waiting,
Stuffy heat unabating.

Then the welcoming smile:
"Sorry you've been waiting a while".
"Come and lie over here on the bed.
Your wife can sit there instead".
Then the careful examination,
Followed by patient explanation.
Time for me to ask questions
About treatment for infections.

After the warmth of encouragement,
The chill of a further appointment.

The next poem 'Swine Flu' had a surprising reaction from one reader: "You should not poke fun at such a serious matter". However, for me humour helped to cope with my own vulnerability to the virus with a compromised immune system. The last two lines have become a much-quoted proverb in our family:

"Meanwhile, don't let the future fear
Spoil the joy today of being here!"

Swine Flu

The lurid slide of the virus filled the screen,
Alarmist predictions "Pandemic!" could be seen.
Mexico's catastrophic export,
Or maybe an Asian or US import?
Dramatic banner headlines. Are they in error,
Or is this Swine Flu a new Black Death terror?
Masks won't protect, nor an anti-viral
That reverses symptoms from a terminal spiral.
Government gives advice about destroying tissues
Wiping surfaces and hygiene issues.
So watch out for symptoms: fever, sneezes,
Headaches, bronchial wheezes.
If we feel like warmed up death,
Or on our very last aching breath,
Gulp two paracetamol down,
Call the doctor from the town.
Rest up, read the paper in your bed
About economic gloom, how bankers misled!
But meanwhile, don't let the future fear
Spoil the joy today of being here!

Now I share a series of poems that are more personal, in the hope they may be of interest or help to readers. 'Scans: The Giant Polo' is a way of using humour to express feelings of anxiety about a CT scan and what it might reveal. In the event after a long wait I was told the scan was clear. What a relief. Then I was told later that on closer examination I had a tumour that would lead to a major operation to remove a ureter and kidney to prevent any cancer 'seeding'.

Writing poetry has been a kind of self-therapy,[18] a way of expressing my feelings, coming to terms, coping with disease and anxiety. I have smiled at aspects of

[18] See e.g. http://www.poetryspace.co.uk/
(accessed 20th March 2012)

these experiences, and found I can laugh at myself.[19]

Scans: The Giant Polo

"Put on a hospital gown",
She said with an I.T. frown.
After struggling behind my back
Tying laces (I lacked the knack!),
I had to drink lots of H2O
So much so, I just had to go!
"Lie on your back, feet up to here,"
A giant polo filled me with fear.
(I hope I come out in mint condition
With several years in remission).
"Just a small prick in your arm"
"A warm feeling will do no harm".
Then while they withdraw from range
Machine-like noises sound quite strange.
I'm bombarded with alien rays
Which uncover my secrets on their displays.
I hope it will not be long to wait
Before the consultant reveals my fate.

---

[19] Julia Darling and Cynthia Fuller, ed. *The Poetry Cure* (Newcastle: Bloodaxe Books, 2005), p11

"I believe that poetry can help to make you better. Poetry is essential, not a frill or a nicety. It comes to all of us when we most need it. As soon as we are in any kind of crisis, or anguish, that is when we reach for poetry, or find ourselves writing a poem for the first time.

I am currently 'Fellow in Health and Literature' in the English School of Newcastle University. I have been exploring how creative writing, particularly poetry, can be used in a health context. I work with doctors and patients, and run workshops for the growing numbers of people who are interested in the healing powers of poetry.

I got involved with this kind of work through my own experience. I have advanced breast cancer, and poetry is what keeps me afloat. Without writing and reading poems, my journey through chemotherapy and radiotherapy, and the general ups and down of illness, would have been unthinkable."

Here is an earlier example of using gentle humour to cope with embarrassing conditions. This raised a smile with a hospital urology department, but for me it was a way of coping.[20]

A Sample of Verse…

Our doctors are polite, never rude,
Or even a 'tad' vulgar or crude:
"We need a lab sample for analysis.
(Not a half bucket full of 'I wish'!)
Just pee in the wee pot
Without spilling the lot.
Avoid contaminating the inside
Or dribbling down the backside.
A clear flowing stream
Is the urologist's dream!"
Hopefully the Lab will say, 'All clear'
To flush away pathological fear.

In 'Faith Through All the Changing Scenes of Life', I smile at myself: the sureness and arrogance of youth, and the previous certainties which I now call into question.

---

[20] See e.g. Gwyneth Lewis, *The Health of Poetry*, Julia Phelps Lecture, Radcliffe Gymnasium, Harvard University, Cambridge, MA, United States, 2nd December 2008 http://www.radcliffe.edu/events/calendar_2008lewis.aspx

"What distinguishes the poet from the rest of the population is that they regularly and voluntarily submit themselves to a state of mind which most people, aside from monks, will avoid like the plague. Not only do poets choose to inhabit this difficult psychic terrain, over far more rewarding pastimes, they develop artistic and emotional strategies which turn this apparently unpromising place into a highly rewarding landscape. I would argue that the poet's value to society primarily lies in his or her resilience in the face of dread, blankness, lack of meaning, in the insistence on shaping something forceful, energetic and delightful out of it. These artistic strategies are the very ones which can get one out of depression."

Recalling the ages and stages of life can somehow bring coherence and meaning to one's biography through smiling eyes.

Faith: Through all the changing scenes of life

When I was just 'Sweet Sixteen'
I thought I'd got it sorted.
In my rapture, pre-millennial
Theology was undistorted:
Clearly Dispensational.
But then by nineteen
I learned of 'J', and 'P' and 'D',
And the problem of Gospel sources.
We relied on F.F. Bruce and IVP
To counter 'critical' forces.
Then by the time I was twenty-three,
I'd read a lot, (I thought),
And taught R.E.
('Honest To God', is that now read,
Or is John Hick ruling instead?).
Now at thirty, dry, 'Surely there's more
As our minister clearly saw.'
(Before the Great Reversal) I had sought
Relief from doubt (and liberal thought).
The Holy Spirit's Baptism
And powerful charism
Released worship and praise
Service and confidence in many ways.
By forty I appreciated
A balance negotiated
Between 'Spirit' and 'Word',
And tested the sermons I had heard.
In my 50's I began to question
My literal Genesis interpretation
As I learned integration
Of other forms of truth
With the Bible reading of my youth.
A World view: Creation, Fall, and Redemption:

God created all reality without exception.
In my sixties I realised human beings are frail
As the health of my twenties began to fail.
There is more time for reflecting,
Enjoying grandchildren and recollection.
"Through all the changes scenes of life
In trouble and in joy
The praises of my God shall still
My heart and tongue employ."

In this next poem 'Check-up', I give access into my experience as a patient through humour. Writing about the events of the day some how helps to reduce the stress, dissipate the emotional strain. Writing can help absorb experience into one's life before filing the trauma away safely. Writing has helped me come to terms with ill health and treatment.[21]

I hoped 'Check-up' might also give health care professionals in a urology department insight into a patient's perspective of procedures that are routine for them, but life-changing for patients.

Check-up
Six a.m. alarm.
Must keep calm;
Take it steady,
To be waiting ready
For a lift for a 7.15 check-in.
(What time does NHS begin?).
7.20 sitting, waiting,
Talking, writing nervously.
"You are fourth on the list" (hopefully).

---

[21] See e.g. the helpful website
http://www.poetrytherapy.org/articles/pt.htm
And Caroline Cordon 2011 http://carolyn-
poeticpause.blogspot.com/2011/01/poetry-as-therapy.html
http://www.nccata.org/poetry_therapy.htm
(accessed 29/12/2011)

"We telephoned two days ago
Several times, but missed you.
You were out you know."
"We left a message on your phone."
"Sorry you had a little moan."
"The consultant works in the morning."
(To patients 'privately' conforming?)
It is the August Bank Holiday,
So extend your patience in a tolerant way.
"Please change in here,
But have no fear,
I know it's really a loo,
And free from bacteria too.
We need a urine sample."
(A litre will be ample).
If you're in the know
Turn on the tap to increase the flow!
A swab poked up your nose
To detect MRSA I suppose.
'We'll check your groin for e-coli
Or a rarer broccoli bacilli'.
'You can sit in the waiting room':
Just feel the anxiety and the gloom;
The TV weather chattering to itself,
While we wonder about our health.
A cheerful voice ended my concern,
"No need to fret. It's now your turn."
I ambled obediently following the nurse,
And lay there exposed for all to see.
For medics it's another cystoscopy.
Just pretend you're having a wee.
"Ah there's a tumour I can see."

And so we face another round
Of treatment on familiar ground.

Writing about situations of discomfort, pain and personal feelings in ill-health or depression can become introspective, negative and a morbid pre-occupation. It can supplement and deepen depressive feelings. I have written verse about hurt feelings when rejected and passed-over, and about pre-occupations of the mind with darker thoughts. One can allow negative or critical thoughts to swirl around in a deepening vortex. Then a darker mind-set can sweep a person along as in a river, out of their depth towards a waterfall of negativity and depression.

In contrast, writing with humour can be edifying, lifting the spirits. It looks beyond the latent morbidity of situations, focusing on the more positive or optimistic. Writing can be a distraction, a kind of catharsis, a self-cognitive therapy.[22]

I hoped this next verse might make readers smile in identity. Two hospital physiotherapists visiting my ward laughed when they read it. It gives insight into patients' anxieties, and the un-spoken and spoken interplay between the medic and patient. Thoughts were filtered or disguised in communication between patient and medic that social psychologists love to explore. Perhaps it also illustrates the importance of getting below the surface, the apparent, to the hidden but more real meanings in the interaction of conversation.

Physiotherapy: Getting Back To Work!

"Hello, how are you today?"
"Oh, not too bad, I'm okay."
(Well, if I'm speaking truthfully,
I'm low, and aching actually,
And I've just been told a tumour

---

[22] For catharsis see:
http://en.wikipedia.org/wiki/Catharsis#Therapeutic_uses, and also see:
http://www.netdoctor.co.uk/diseases/depression/cognitivet herapy_000439.htm   (both accessed 29 Dec 2011.)

Has re-appeared, so my humour
Is subdued, a little glum…
That's the truth, about the sum.)
"How have the exercises been?"
(They created pain, so I wasn't keen).
"Oh, I made a start, a stretch or two."
(A pain in the neck, if more than a few).
"Well let's take a look, see how you're doing."
(Does my deodorant need renewing?)
"Show me doing your exercises.
There's more here this sheet devises."
"You are now much more mobile,
So I'll massage for a while."
(Why do I feel so shy, so ill
At ease while lying still?).

The poem reveals a patient's hidden thoughts and embarrassment with a smile.

A visit to the doctor's surgery where a medic showed concern about my blood pressure prompted the poem *High Pressure*. It deals with the anxiety and pressure of getting to a surgery with a touch of humour that relieved the stress:

High Pressure

Plenty of time
I shouldn't be late;
A traffic jam to navigate,
Several 'red lights'
Where we had to wait;
Find a space to park
Without getting in a state;
Check-in with a queue
Sit down to learn my fate.

"Your blood pressure
Is raised, a little high"
White coat syndrome:
I'm wondering why!

Recently our local hospital proposed raising car parking charges dramatically to offset government financial cuts. I wrote the next two poems to the hospital administration hoping that the humour might have a sufficiently sharp cutting edge to change the proposal. These are examples of harder-hitting satirical[23] or ironic humour I have used, which expresses my annoyance. 'Patients First' is the motif, the banner, expressing the hospital's values, but the raise in car park costs seemed to work against this. The expression 'Taxing the frail and sick' has brought some smiles, but I hope the poem illuminated the collision between values and economics, between ethics and policy.

"Patients First"

You have a noble motif
That is of course if
Raising the parking fee
Is not just accountancy
To make some money quick
By taxing the frail and sick.

"You should catch the 61 bus.
Stop creating all this fuss."
"Yes, they're hourly, we often wait,
So we'll arrive at our appointment late."

The huge percentage rise
Seems neither fair nor wise.
It's the financial implication
That needed further consultation.

---

[23] See *Laughter and The Political Landscape*, Lageson S, Erensu S, Green K. 2012 for a discussion of humour about politics and politicians. http://thesocietypages.org/roundtables/ (accessed 20th February 2012)

Raising The Speculation

Instead of patients punishing
And visitors discouraging,
I have been wondering
Whether in your pondering
Planning and budgeting
You had been discussing
A more positively enterprising
Way of filling and replacing
The gaps in your funding
To a higher plain transporting
Such as imaginative marketing
Your premises and catering
Private sector consulting
Executive health screening
Stress and trauma counselling
In-service training
For education and teaching
Professional expertise exporting
A manager organizing
Their own salary raising
Entrepreneurially generating
Income for 'Patients First' serving?

The poems did not alter the proposal. I noted in an e-mail that the hospital governors disagreed with the director's decision, and later saw a notice in a hospital lift that there were concessions organised for regular users of the car park. Perhaps they had listened to the outcry in the local press? When parking for appointments I feel a mischievous sense of victory when I can drive out of the car park free because the barrier pole is raised in a mal-function of the mechanism!

I hope my writing continues to raise a smile, and lift spirits. Seeing the humorous dimension in painful circumstances is a way of helping me to cope. I think it was Goethe who said, "I never had a great suffering but

I made it into a poem." Turning an experience into verse can be a way of 'off-loading' the emotion, a way of processing and coming to terms with the experience, looking for light at the end of a dark tunnel. In a strange way the process of writing, looking down upon myself at my situation somehow helps me turn my attention away from myself to take an interest in what is happening around me, and the people involved. We can then empathise with others, and raise their faith and spirits.

This prayer was written for a colleague who had been diagnosed with breast cancer. It was warmly received:

> Lord,
> I'm praying this morning
> For release from anxiety,
> Protection from panic
> And the paralysis of fear:
> The renewing of my mind
> In my anger and
> The darkness of depression;
> And for the practice
> Of 'Thanks-living'
> For all the blessings
> In spite of everything.
>
> Help me to focus
> On priorities,
> Take joy in the familiar
> And in serving others,
> Express my love,
> Think more of You,
> To escape the
> Tyranny of the 'I'.

I am hoping that this chapter may contribute in a small way to the literature about writing poetry as a form of therapy.

The final poem for this chapter on Poetry and Humour was a winning entry for Central Bedfordshire Libraries Poetry Competition 2011 on the theme of 'Games':

The Beautiful Game

We don't have names
For the kind of Games
Participants play
For eye-watering pay:
Body tattooing,
Colour shampooing,
Luxury shopping,
Exotic travelling,
Cars competing,
Petulant protesting,
Diving, pretending,
The right to refuse
To play in the news.
Why do we still pay
For 'games' in this way?

The poem really speaks for itself about some professional footballers in the UK. It is a poem of mild protest.

References

Andreas G. (superbly illustrated by Guy Parker-Rees) 2000 onwards. *Rumble in The Jungle, Commotion in The Ocean* & *The Lion Who Wanted Love*. London: Orchard Books.

Cordon C. 2011 http://carolyn-poeticpause.blogspot. com/2011/01/poetry-as-therapy.html

Darling J. and Cynthia Fuller C. 2005, ed. *The Poetry Cure* (Newcastle: Bloodaxe Books), p11

Holy Bible. The New International Version.1979. Cambridge: C.U.P.

http://www.postwritersgroup.com/goodman.htm (accessed 5July 2011)

http://www.radcliffe.edu/events/calendar_2008lewis.aspx

http://www.bbc.co.uk/bbctrust/news/press_releases/2 008/october/russell_brand_show.shtml (accessed 18 May 2011)

http://www.poetryspace.co.uk/

http://www.poetrytherapy.org/articles/pt.htm

Lageson S., Erensu S., Green K. 2012. *Laughter and The Political Landscape* http://thesocietypages.org/roundtables/ (accessed 20 February 2012)

Lewis G. *The Health of Poetry*, Julia Phelps Lecture, Radcliffe Gymnasium, Harvard University, Cambridge, MA, United States, 2nd December 2008

Moore P.1989 *Disarming The Secular Gods* Leicester UK: IVP

Pemberton M. 2011 'Doctors Must Laugh in the Face of Death'. *The Daily Telegraph*. Sept 29th, 2011. London. Telegraph Media Group.

Smith, M., Kemp G., and Sega J. *Laughter the Best Medicine* at: http://www.helpguide.org/life/humor_laughter_health.htm   (accessed 17/5/2011)

Taylor K.N. *The Living Bible* 1974. London: Coverdale House Pub.

Questions for Reflection:

1. What are some of the positive effects of humour in your community or society?

2. What would be an example of a negative effect of humour?

3. How has writing humorous poetry helped the author?

4. Which of these poems did you like the most?

5. How can poetry be a kind of therapy?

6. What place might humorous poetry have in your situation, ministry or professional practice?

CHAPTER 3

POETRY and PROPHECY

This chapter shares the author's thinking about poetry and prophecy. It addresses four questions:

1. What is the connection between poetry and prophecy generally?
2. What is the relationship between 'prophet' and 'poetry' in the Old Testament?
3. How are the role of the prophet and purposes of prophecy different in the New Testament?
4. In what way may we speak of poetry now in our own time as being prophetic?

Photo: Reflections at Whipsnade by the author

The poet may have to stand apart from the community to think and reflect. The prophet needs to stand alone in the presence of God to hear from him. Both may be considered odd or be rejected by their peers, but the ripples of their words can spread out far and wide.

POETRY and PROPHECY

This chapter is an account of the author's thinking about Poetry and Prophecy, stimulated by his reading about the nature and the genre of poetry and its impact on the reader. The author writes poetry to communicate ideas about the Christian faith. He is particularly interested in how faith can influence actions, and can impact society, so these themes or threads can be seen in his verse.

In musing on some feedback comments from readers, and reflecting about whether writing can be a ministry in a church community, he has pondered over a possible connection between poetry and prophecy. He has wondered what might be the relationship between prophet and poet, and between poetry and prophecy. Is there a parallel, even a close connection between 'prophecy' and 'poetry', between poet and prophet?[1]

When I scan through the Bible, particularly the Old Testament I am impressed with the amount of poetry, song, psalm and lament. On re-reading the Old Testament prophets Jeremiah, then Isaiah, and Lamentations I have been struck with the appearance and forms of writing, such as the text set-out as poetry in large sections[2] rather than prose. The parallelism of

---

[1] After writing this chapter, I came across J.L. Kugel's book *Poetry and Prophecy* in which he explores similar questions more eruditely with his colleague writers.

[2] See helpful article: Kidner D. 1973 Poetry and Wisdom Literature. Introduction. In *The Lion Handbook to the Bible*. Alexander D. & Alexander P. 1973. Berkhamsted: Lion Publishing

structure, (a line repeating the idea of the previous line)[3], imagery, and the music of words is even retained in English translation of the prophet Isaiah:

> "Comfort, comfort my people,
> Says your God,
> Speak tenderly to Jerusalem,
> And proclaim to her
> That her hard service has been completed,
> That her sin has been paid for…
> (Isaiah 40,1-2)

The forms, language, rhythm, and imagery of poetry are important means of communication in scripture, particularly in the Hebrew Prophets. So, I have been stimulated to address these four questions:

1. 'What is the connection between poetry and prophecy generally?'
2. 'What is the relationship between prophet and poetry in the Old Testament?'
3. 'How are the role of the prophet and the purposes of prophecy different in the New Testament?'
4. 'In what way can we speak of poetry now as being "prophetic"?'

An immediate semantic problem in the world of Religious Studies that I have inhabited in Education is 'What do people mean by the words 'prophet' and 'prophecy'? In everyday speech, in what we hear on the television, or if you ask someone in the street or at the school gates, 'What is a prophet, or prophecy?', the answer might be 'Someone who foretells the future'. Vox pops, and current ideas, might include 'It's like science fiction that comes true'. Some people might say that admired leaders or great figures like Mother

---

[3] for explanation see:
http://jewishencyclopedia.com/view.jsp?artid=67&letter=P

Theresa,[4] Gladys Aylward,[5] Martin Luther King,[6] Nelson Mandela,[7] The Dalai Lama,[8] or Desmond Tutu[9] could be called Prophets of the modern era. (We all have our favourite great leaders, or exemplars). People who are admired, voices who have spoken into social situations with power and insight inspiring a generation with their thought and actions might be called prophets in this sense, in our own twenty-first century too.

There have been seers[10] and prophets[11] down through history who have left their oracles, some of which have verse forms or poetic styles of writing. Wikipedia is a helpful source for illustrations and examples of these seers. People have consulted wise women[12] for guidance and healing, seers and fore-seers to enquire into future events.[13]

Religious founders like Muhammad, holy men and writers of scriptures have been called 'prophets' and given the highest respect.[14] There is no doubt about the poetic language of the scriptures of Islam, Hinduism, and Sikhism, (the Qur'an, the Bhavagad Gita, or parts of

---

[4] http://nobelprize.org/nobel_prizes/peace/laureates/1979/teresa-bio.html (accessed 27/4/2010)

[5] http://www.heroesofhistory.com/page46.html (accessed 27/4/2010)

[6] http://martinlutherking.org/

[7] http://www.nelsonmandela.org/index.php

[8] The Dalai Lama. (Tenzin Gyatso) 2007. *Mind in Comfort and Ease.* Somerville. USA: Wisdom Pub.

[9] Tutu D. 2004. *God Has A Dream.* London: Rider (Imprint of Ebury Press).

[10] http://en.wikipedia.org/wiki/Clairvoyance (accessed 27/4/2011)

[11] http://en.wikipedia.org/wiki/Prophet

[12] http://en.wikipedia.org/wiki/Wise_Woman

[13] See Haslam G.2009 p.54 for distinguishing genuine prophecy.

[14] For a cautionary view see Gabriel M. A. 2008 *Coffee With the Prophet.* Casselberry, Florida: Gabriel Publishing; and Yousef M.H. 2011. *Son of Hamas.* Milton Keynes: Authentic.

the Guru Granth Sahib). Even to those of us who cannot read the original languages, the English translations of these prophets' words reflect the imagery, assonance, verse forms, rhythm and colour of the original.

The adhan, the Muslim call to prayer, rings out from mosque minarets across the Middle East. The poetic cadences of the Arabic are reflected in English translation, "God is most great, God is most great… come to prayer, come to prayer, come to success, come to success…" [15]

Poetic imagery, and parallelism is retained in the English quotation from the Qur'an:

'We sent Jesus Son of Mary,
Confirming the Law that had come before him;
We sent him the gospel,
Wherein was guidance and light,
And a confirmation of the Law,
A guidance and a warning to those who fear God'
Surah 5,46. [16] [17]

Even in English translation we catch the poetry of Krishna speaking to Arjuna in the Hindu text Bhavagad Gita when he says, "There was never a time when I did not exist":

Know this Atman
Unborn undying,
Never ceasing,
Never beginning,
Deathless, birthless,

---

[15] Quoted in Keene M. 1997. *Examining Four Religions*. Hong Kong: HarperCollins)

[16] Quoted in Kendrick R. 1989. *Islam*. Oxford: Heinemann Educational

[17] See also Surah 1, El Fatiha; Surah 99 The Earthquake; Al-Zalzala Surah 82. The Cleaving. Al-Infitar Zayid M.Y.1980 The Quran. Beirut, Lebanon: Dar Al-Chora

Unchanging for ever.
How can it die
The death of the body? [18] [19].

Here is an extract of The Sikh morning prayer by Guru Nanak written in verse:

Hearing the Word, we plumb the depths of virtue,
Hearing the Word, we rise to the status of sages and
  kings,
Hearing the Word, the path is lit for the blind,
Hearing the Word, the fathomless is fathomed.
Says Nanak, the devout enjoy eternal bliss,
Hearing the Word, banishes all suffering and sin[20] [21]

We can claim there is a relationship between poetry and prophet. At the most basic level poetry can be the medium of the message. It is the form of language through which the prophet or holy person speaks. The Prophets and their disciples have left believers with poetry, and the rhythm of oral tradition, no doubt to assist transmission and memorisation. However at a deeper level poetry as a genre has a way of speaking, the so-called 'Heineken effect' ('reaching parts others don't reach'). It has an impact on the reader with colourful and vivid images. It compresses ideas. The meaning can baffle the reader, then 'explode' on meditation. It can impact the mind, arouse emotions and move the will to action.

It is interesting to me as a Christian that God who is The Logos, The Word, should choose to make himself known through spoken and written words. But not only through description, historical narrative, teaching in

---

[18] http://www.bhagavad-gita.us/ (accessed 26/4/2011)
[19] Quoted p.54-55 Burke T.P.2004. *The Major Religions*. Oxford: Blackwell
[20] p.114 Burke T.P. 2004. *The Major Religions*: Oxford. Blackwell
[21] http://granthsahib.com/ (accessed 26/4/2011)

prose, through proverbs and Wisdom literature, and letters, but also through poetry, songs, laments, and Psalms.[22] Is there something more to the genre other than just the structure and beauty of the medium?

Poets write to express a range of feelings, thoughts, and impressions within structures, and forms of verse, employing rich language, vivid metaphor and imagery. They capture scenes or portray events. They make social analysis or comment. They express humour, satire, and faith and doubt. Poetry is not one genre but a range of types of writing: expressive and creative; descriptive; wistful; evocative; informative; didactic; confrontational and so on.

Furthermore poets also speak of the 'inspiration' of ideas coming deep from within themselves, or from 'outside'. A web-search on 'poetic inspiration' reveals a range of understandings of this idea, from the inspiration of nature through to the pagan understanding, and occult inspiration.[23] [24]

Denise Levertov in speaking on 'Work and Inspiration: Inviting The Muse' comments:

> 'Poems come into being in two ways. There are those which are – or used to be – spoken of as *inspired* poems which seem to appear out of nowhere, complete or very nearly so; which are written quickly without conscious premeditation, taking the writer by surprise... Such poems often seem to have that aura of authority, of the incontrovertible, the air being mysteriously lit from within their substance...

---

[22] http://70030.netministry.com/images/TypesofGenresinthe Bible.pdf (accessed 2/5/2011)

[23] http://www.google.co.uk/#sclient=psy&hl=en&source= hp&q=poetic+inspiration&aq=0&aqi=g3g-v2&aql=&oq= &pbx=1&fp=495eca51a8ef0dd

[24] For further interpretations of poetic inspiration see Wikipedia entries on 'Awen', on 'Robert Graves', 'The White Goddess'

some of their work requires labour… Many drafts and revisions…[25]

The great prophets of the Old Testament were inspired in quite a different way. They were not just expressing the creativity of the human mind and spirit. They brought consolation, inspired hope in dark times, challenged political leaders in the present situation, and pronounced judgement, but they are not just expressing thoughts from their 'depths'. They speak of the future, things to come, but not just from their own speculation, insight, or supra-human vision.

The defining characteristic of Old Testament prophets is that they claimed to speak the words of God.[26] They are his mouthpiece. There is revelation of the mind of God, through people who had been in the council chamber of the Almighty. They spoke "Thus says the Lord."[27] Jeremiah[28] is able to say with assurance, "This is what the Lord says." The word of the Lord, 'came to him'. He had a dramatic call to the prophetic role:

---

[25] Levertov D. 1969 in *A Field Guide to Contemporary Poetry and Poetics*. Ed. Freibert S. , Walker D., Young D. 1997. Ohio U.S: Oberlin College Press

[26] As Peisker comments, 'the Hebrew word for prophet 'nabi' is usually derived from Akkad. vb nabu to call, to proclaim… "the OT prophet is a proclaimer of the word, called by God to warn, exhort, comfort, teach and counsel, bound to God alone…" ('prophet' in *New International Dictionary of New Testament Theology Vol. 3*).

[27] Jewett P.K. 1974. Prophecy. In *The New Dictionary of The Christian Church* Ed. Douglas J.D. 1974. Exeter: Paternoster.

Asamoah-Gyadu K. 2007. Prophecy. *Dictionary of Mission Theology*. Ed. Corrie J. Nottingham: IVP.

Motyer J.A. 1965. Prophecy. *The New Bible Dictionary*. Ed. Douglas J.D. London. IVF.

[28] Jeremiah 21,1; 22,1; 1,4-9;

"Before I formed you in the womb I knew you,
Before you were born I set you apart;
I appointed you as a prophet to the nations".
"Ah, Sovereign Lord… I do not know how to speak;
I am only a child"…
"You must go to everyone I send you to and say
   whatever I command you.
Do not be afraid of them, for I am with you and will
   rescue you"…
Then the Lord reached out his hand and touched my
   mouth and said to me,
"Now, I have put my words in your mouth."[29]

As Moses[30] before him, Isaiah[31] had a dramatic, impacting call to be a prophet, (a life-changing vision in the Temple). Some of these prophets would not have chosen this role, some even resisting, but the 'hand of the Lord' falls on them. They sometimes speak under compulsion. The Spirit of God 'rests on', or 'clothes them'. These seers had privileged access to the mind of God, to his counsel through revelations, dreams, visions and insight. They communicate through speech, symbols, allegories, dramatic actions, and in poetic forms the very mind and words of Almighty God. There are severe warnings about presuming to speak in God's name.[32]

How were the Hebrews to evaluate prophecy? What was the ultimate test of prophecy?

"If what a prophet proclaims in the name of the Lord does not take place or come true, that is a message the Lord has not spoken. That prophet has spoken presumptuously. Do not be afraid of him"[33]

---

[29] Jeremiah 1,6-9
[30] Exodus chapter 3
[31] Isaiah chapter 6
[32] Deuteronomy 18,20; Ezekiel ch.13
[33] Deuteronomy 18,21

The Hebrew prophets brought revelation, vision for the nation, guidance in historical settings, critique of powerful people in high positions, and pronouncement of judgement. They called the people back to faith in God and loyalty to the covenant.[34]

It would take a foolishly bold person to make presumptuous claims in our own historical time to be prophets in the Old Testament sense. I am very cautious and questioning when anyone claims to be a prophet or speaks in a church prefacing their pronouncement with, "Thus saith Lord". By what authority might they claim this?

Similarly, I think it would be mistaken to claim that our poetry is 'prophetic' in this Old Covenant sense. I feel we should be hesitant to claim our poetry is even 'prophetic', or has a 'prophetic edge' in the sense I have been describing. As I discuss later we hope and pray that God will speak through verse, enlightening minds, moving emotions, and perhaps, revealing things, and building faith. Others must be the judge of the impact of our poetry. Perhaps the Holy Spirit may use poems in His work and speak though them. There is no room for hubris.[35] Modesty needs to clothe the poet, but here I am anticipating my final question.

So yes, the prophets or their disciples can be poets [36] as illustrated by the Hebrew Prophets of the eighth century BC, Amos and Hosea. The words of God are expressed in poetic forms with rhythm.

---

[34] See e.g. an older writer H.Wheeler Robinson 1956 'The Prophetic Consciousness' in *The Religious Ideas of The Old Testament*

[35] "excessive pride or self-confidence" OED

[36] See Kugel J. 1981 *The Idea of Biblical Poetry*, and particularly Alter R. 1985 *The Art of Biblical Poetry* for a much fuller discussion.

The words of Amos:
This is what the LORD says:
 "For three sins of Damascus,
  even for four, I will not relent.
Because she threshed Gilead
  with sledges having iron teeth,
4 I will send fire on the house of Hazael
  that will consume the fortresses of Ben-Hadad.
5 I will break down the gate of Damascus;
  I will destroy the king who is in the Valley of Aven
and the one who holds the sceptre in Beth Eden.
  The people of Aram will go into exile to Kir,"
    says the LORD.[37]

The poetry in Hosea:

 "I will heal their waywardness
  and love them freely,
   for my anger has turned away from them.
5 I will be like the dew to Israel;
  he will blossom like a lily.
Like a cedar of Lebanon
  he will send down his roots;
6 his young shoots will grow.
His splendour will be like an olive tree,
  his fragrance like a cedar of Lebanon.
7 People will dwell again in his shade;
  they will flourish like the grain,
they will blossom like the vine—
  Israel's fame will be like the wine of Lebanon.
8 Ephraim, what more have I to do with idols?
  I will answer him and care for him.
I am like a flourishing juniper;
  your fruitfulness comes from me."[38]

[37] Amos Chapter 1. N.I.V. 1993 Cambridge. Univ: Cambridge
[38] Hosea 14,4-8 http://www.biblegateway.com/passage/
?search=Hosea%2014&version=NIV

The ancient prophet/poets of the Bible express and inspire worship, and speak to people in their time. Moreover, they can speak to us now in our time, about situations in life of pain, despair and anxiety.

They also speak of things to come in their own historical context, or of the longer-term future. Zechariah speaks of nations being gathered against Jerusalem.[39] Micah speaks about the 'last days', and the dream of universal peace.[40] Matthew quotes prophecies fulfilled by the Nativity. (Mat. 1,23; 2,6; 2,15; 2,18;). Isaiah 53 and Psalm 22 are widely quoted to be foretelling events of the life of Jesus, and the words of Jesus when He was on the cross. Isaiah 65, 17-26 speaks of the New Heavens and Earth.

Poetry with its rich language, metaphor, analogy, and verse forms is the vehicle for communicating the prophets' messages. The rhythm, assonance and parallelism may have helped transmission and memory of the prophets' words. The literary devices help the meaning to impact explosively. However, it is the message, the very words of God, that give access to the divine mind that is ascendant and most important. It is the meaning rather than the form that has priority, although of course they are inextricably linked.

The next two poems were part of a series of verses that were the outcome of listening to sermons on Jeremiah, reading about the prophet, and reflecting about the content, historical background and the process of the prophecy.

Jeremiah's background:
(Reflections by the Author)

In the darkest decade
Two boys were born.
King Manasseh had made

---

[39] Zechariah 14.
[40] Micah 4,1-5.

Policies Judah learned to mourn:
Involving human sacrifice, idolatry,
Black arts and necromancy.
His deliberate reversal and apostasy
Left the people damaged spiritually.

Jeremiah was born in 648,
The outspoken prophet to the nation state.
He received threats and rejection,
Wrestled with God feeling dejection.
He proclaimed the message, and persisted
But the rebellious people resisted.
Judgment came through Nebuchadnezzar,
Defeat and Exile, another sermon's chapter.

Jeremiah

(A meditation on a sermon)

Prophet in the reforms of Josiah,
In the reigns of Jehoiakim and Zedekiah,
Kings of Judah 6-7th Centuries B.C.;
But what's this to do with me?

Jeremiah was called to speak
Even though he felt so weak,
Chosen to address a wayward nation,
To express God's indignation
For wickedness in forsaking
God, worshiping idols of their making.

God reached out His commanding hand
Touched his lips to address the Land.
Almond tree and 'pot-boiling' vision,
'Coming judgment' was his mission.
"Don't be terrified", "I am with you",
"Stand and speak", "I will rescue".

So what's the relevance for us today?
We have a message in a similar way.
Called by God, given a Great Commission,
Warning of judgment is part of our mission.
We have his promise on Scripture's page

"I will be with you to the end of the age."

Now we must address our third question: 'How are the role of the Prophet and the purposes of prophecy different in the New Testament?' In the New Testament Jesus is the archetype 'prophet', priest and king. The writer to the Hebrews says that God spoke through the prophets but 'in these last days he has spoken to us by his Son'.[41] There is in one sense, no need in the Church Age for Old Testament-type prophets speaking 'Thus says the Lord', because Jesus is 'The Word', the revelation of God. "The Word became flesh, and we have seen his glory" the theme of John's Prologue.[42] We have the Word of God, the Old and New Testaments.

In the New Testament there were Prophets as an office alongside the Apostles, (like Agabus).[43] Paul describes them as one of Christ's gifts to the Church.[44] The Christian Church was said to be built on the foundations of the Apostles and Prophets. Prophecy according to St Paul is about speaking words of 'strengthening, encouragement and comfort' in corporate worship.[45]

The word 'revelation' is associated with prophecy in Paul's teaching:

> Two or three prophets should speak, and others should weigh carefully what is said. And if a **revelation** comes to someone who is sitting down, the first speaker should stop'[46]

'But if an unbeliever ...comes in while everybody is prophesying, he will be convinced by all that he is a

---

[41] Hebrews 1,1-4

[42] St. John chapter 1

[43] Acts 11,27-28

[44] Ephesians 4,7-13

[45] 1 Corinthians chapter 15

[46] 1 Corinthians 14, 29-33

sinner and will be judged by all, and the secrets of his heart will be laid bare'[47]

Wayne Grudem comments,

'God may suddenly bring to mind, or…may impress on someone's consciousness in such a way that the person senses that it is from God'.

'As far as we can tell, all New Testament prophecy was based on this kind of spontaneous prompting from the Holy Spirit…, unless a person receives a spontaneous 'revelation' from God, there is no prophecy'[48]

He goes on to distinguish prophecy from teaching, arguing the latter has more authority than the former. Prophecy is not just powerful preaching, although preaching may contain re-revelation, and conviction by the Holy Spirit. Preachers can speak powerfully to individuals and uncover situations or issues of which they can have no personal knowledge, but they are recognised by the hearer. Grudem also makes clear that any prophesying must be subservient to the revelation of Scripture.

Now I want address my final question, 'In what way can we speak of poetry now as being "prophetic"?' In a lesser sense, the poet may speak words that strengthen faith, that comfort, or encourage. They are not necessarily revelation from God, but they could be. Some poems may have what might be loosely termed 'a prophetic edge' or flavour in this sense: the words may have particular relevance, meaning and application to individuals' lives. You may hear the phrase, 'that poem spoke to me', or 'I was deeply moved by that poem'. Maybe it was instrumental in strengthening faith, giving encouragement at a difficult time, touching emotions or

---

[47] 1 Corinthians 14, 24-25
[48] P.1056-1058 *Systematic Theology*

giving words of comfort. Poems can also teach us, reveal truth, leading to understanding and insight.[49]

Poems have a way of 'speaking' to individual readers. They can strengthen faith and personal resolve to face life's challenges. They can encourage and console in dark times. Poetry can 'speak' in a deep way to readers.[50]

It is possible for the poet to publish their verses for dubious or mixed motives to be recognised or to be self-assertive. The author recognizes this in himself on occasions. The Industry has its own phrase, 'Vanity Publishing'. Christian poets may need to reflect about their motives.[51]

This next poem had a way of addressing personally, a way of speaking for one reader who attended an Easter Sunday Service. It seemed to sum-up and give an 'action replay' of her experience of reflection about the Easter story.

The congregation brought flowers to attach to a wire framework of a cross, transforming it into a colourful symbol of the Resurrection. Poems can 'speak' or have impact for some readers but be ignored, passed over, or have no impact on others. This poem may have little impact on some readers. Some people tell me they have little interest or patience with poems, but others respond warmly because it catches the experience and worship of the occasion. The poem can express feelings readers find difficult to articulate.

Writing poetry can involve a playfulness with words. I made a cross structure with some words from Isaiah 33 that were particularly meaningful to me. I hoped it

---

[49] See Jackie Hill's poems that have been described as prophetic http://www.linkedin.com/pub/jackie-hill/19/758/741/

[50] The writer finds great encouragement from readers who write giving feed-back on the impact of his poems.

[51] I pray that my words may be a ministry to help, bless, and challenge readers as a channel for God's Spirit.

might 'speak', encourage and build faith in members of my family and for our friends:

The Cross
Stood bare
Brown and bleak
Scarred and stark
Stained with pain
Aching with
Abandonment.
Then all gathered brought a flower gift,
Waiting reverently, attaching gently,
Gradually transforming the cruelty of the Cross
Into a glorious celebration of Resurrection.
Tributes of love were expressed:
Yellow daffodils,
Perfumed Narcissi,
White and fragrant
Lily of The Valley,
Green palm rich
In memories:
A Magnificat.
A garland of praise!

Oh Lord,
Be gracious
To Us.
We long
For You.
Be our strength
Every Morning,
Our salvation in the time of distress.
The LORD is exalted for He dwells on high.
He will fill Zion with justice and righteousness.
He will be a sure foundation for your times,
A rich store
of Salvation
And Wisdom
And Knowledge:
The fear of
The LORD
Is the KEY
To this
TREASURE
(Isaiah 33)

Some poems do have a way of 'speaking' to individual readers, or of evoking a powerful memory. The poet, who like the prophet may feel a 'burden'[52], communicates the message, but has no control over its effect, and indeed may never know what impact it has had or the interpretation that has been made. There is a sense in which the poet writes what they wish or 'must', in hope and faith, in a similar way to the prophet.

This next poem was written by request for someone who was experiencing 'burn-out'. It had this 'speaking' effect on a reader who was deeply moved and encouraged. Another reader e-mailed that it came 'just at the right time' for her in a busy stressful life.

Lord,
The constant driving,
Incessant striving,
The expectations
And justifications…
I can't keep up with
Life's palpitations…

Awaking from a restless night
I've lost the will to face the fight
The 'To Do' list just increasing
Guilt and apathy competing.
I admit an inability to cope.
Life's lost that lustre of a living hope.

Lord,
Where is your 'peace', Shalom today?
Is this just blind acceptance come what may?
I've told others to keep faith and trust still
In whatever happens, good or ill.
I never thought I would make these confessions
Or even pose these disturbing questions.

---

[52] See Michael Card's 2002 *Scribbling in the Sand* where he talks about the 'burden' which he has before composing some songs.

Restore to me the joy of salvation.
Father, send your love and restoration.
Heal my restive spirit, burnt out soul.
Give me the humility of pacing.
I need 'time-outs', wisdom to avoid the racing,
The skill to challenge negative feelings and thoughts
To be released from the tyranny of others' 'ought's'.

Lord,
I need this space to draw refreshment
From Your springs, to recover contentment,
The inspiration and reassurance
That you are here in whatever circumstance.
Come alongside, give that Living Water
Renew my mind and vision whenever they falter.

I have encountered at least four stances toward, or opinions about prophecy,[53] or prophesying in our own time.

1. Prophecy is delusional, wishful thinking, or at worst the exercise of power over the vulnerable or gullible. Any predictive element is dismissed as coincidence, or serendipity. They say, 'Belief in the supernatural has little place in our secular and rational age'.

2. There are phenomena of prophecies, fortune-tellers, seers, and occult powers that are recorded, observable, but not fully understood. Christians may be advised to steer clear of the occult.

---

[53]After completing this chapter I came across Grudem W. 1996 *Are Miraculous Gifts for Today?* This book lays out four viewpoints very clearly for readers in a fair and gracious way.
See also the helpful discussion between Ian Hamilton and Wayne Grudem on 'Prophecy in the Church. Or Not.'
A video: http://www.proctrust.org.uk/blog/2012-02-23/prophecy-in-church-today-or-not-1353
(accessed 25 February 2012).

3. There is what I call a 'low' view of prophecy.[54] Many Christian churches teach that 'there were gifts of prophecy and the office of prophet in New Testament times. We now have God's revelation in Scripture so we do not need prophecy. God speaks into the minds of people through powerful expository preaching of God's Word applied to personal and social situations. The Holy Spirit speaks through the read and preached Word (Bible)'.

One minister explained:

> '(the minister's job) is to spend much of the week carefully considering and praying over the passage with the task of faithfully, accurately and clearly publicly proclaiming the Word of God in all its fullness as Pastors of God's flock; this is the on-going dimension of prophecy in this present gospel era, in my view' [55]

4. Then there are different levels[56] of interpretation that place a higher degree of importance on prophecy (e.g. Charismatic/Pentecostal views). Here is a sense of the view: 'Prophets are Christ's gift to the Church. Prophecy as a gift of the Holy Spirit is encouraged by St Paul. Both are available today for giving Christians vision, insight, comfort, strengthening of faith, and bringing conviction in mission'.

They say that prophecy brings revelation of the mind of God about current situations. It can be delivered as pictures, songs, actions or messages. However, it must be tested and evaluated by Christian leaders and operated in a disciplined and accountable way. It is always to be subservient to, and tested by Scripture.

---

[54] See e.g. Jackman D. 2004. Let's Study 1 Corinthians
[55] In private e-mail to the author about an earlier draft of the chapter.
[56] See e.g. Prior D. 1985/1993. The Message of 1 Corinthians, pp.235-255 for a clear exposition of Paul's Corinthians teaching on prophecy.

Greg Haslam has written a most helpful exposition on prophecy with an extensive bibliography.[57] He explains why he believes prophecy is still available as a gift from God. Then he expands on his understanding of the nature of prophecy today giving illustrations and helpful advice. Prophets can point the way, build hope, and bring the Church foresight and exhortation through inspiration beyond natural abilities alone.[58]

Poetry is the 'maid of honour' not the bride herself. As we have seen at Prince William's and Katherine Middleton's (The Duchess of Cambridge)[59] wedding, the maid of honour Pippa, Katherine's sister has a charm, a beauty, a dignity, and attentiveness of her own[60], but was not the centre of attention.

Poetry can be the medium of prophecy, the structure and form of language in which the prophecy is couched. A revelation could be spoken in poetry. Greg Haslam writes about prophetic songs,

> 'Some came spontaneously, complete with beautiful poetry and inspiring melody; some were carefully composed in private before they were launched in public'[61]

When I went to Shenyang in China I was introduced to Chinese Christian songs that were 'given', just came into the mind, to a lady who farmed while she worked in the fields. She sang the songs to a Western writer who recorded them, and now they are sung by Chinese Christians.

---

[57] Haslam G. 2009. *Moving In The Prophetic*. Oxford: Monarch.
[58] P.38 Haslam G. op. cit. See also Prior D. op.cit
[59] Now the Duke and Duchess of Cambridge
[60] See *The Daily Telegraph* April 30th, 2011. p.6.7, and 19. London. Telegraph Media Group
[61] Greg Haslam 2009 p.147-148

So Haslam's view of prophecy is broader, not limited to revelation in church meetings as is Grudem's.[62] Poetry can 'speak' to the reader, build faith, bring conviction, comfort, or encouragement. The Holy Spirit can use the genre of poetry to speak into our lives, (there is nothing new about this), as He has used the words of hymn-writers down through the years to teach, inspire, challenge and comfort. Indeed, I learned much of my early Christian theology as a child and teenager through hymns and songs. Think of the impact Charles Wesley's[63] hymns have had on Christians. It would not be prophecy in the sense Grudem defines, but might be one aspect of Haslam's 'Moving in The Prophetic'.

Poems designed to alert Christians, or to critique aspects of society, verses applying the teaching of Scripture to current situations might have a 'prophetic edge or dimension'. Poetry can be a means of the Word of God reverberating (to use Jonathan Leeman's expression[64]) through to the reader.

Here are a group of poems which may have this reverberating effect, addressing issues that were current when written. I have circulated them through e-mails and blogs to widen the audience and possible impact.

A Secularist Xmas

The people who walk
In darkness, who talk
Of 'Enlightenment',
With secularist sentiment,

---

[62] But see a thorough exposition in *The Gift of Prophecy*. Grudem W.A. 2000. Wheaton, Illinois, US: Crossway. See also Brian Onken's review of the book and reservations at http://www.equip.org/articles/the-gift-of-prophecy/ (accessed January 22 nd, 2013).

[63] http://gbgm-umc.org/umhistory/wesley/hymns/

[64] www.discerningreader.com/book-reviews/reverberation (accessed 24 Dec 2011)

Would if they were able
Crucify the Christ in the cradle.

No Angels, no heavenly choir;
No Magi in their rich attire;
No Virgin: a myth, merely;
No peace on Earth, clearly.
No sin, so no Messiah to save;
No hope beyond the grave.

Thank God for the Incarnation
For the child who brings Salvation.

The Brokenness of Britain
(On Reading Michael Nazir-Ali's letter to
The Daily Telegraph 5th March 2010)

Cameron's 'Brokenness of Britain'
Is debated by the politician.
The 'Reservoir' is running dry.
The Press is pausing to ask 'Why?'
Refreshing streams have been polluted,
Causes questioned and disputed.
With all our secular social analysis
Political and economic crisis
Do we need to 'unblock those streams'
Revive our spiritual and moral dreams?

As Michael Nazir-Ali wrote
"The moral code", that the columnists' quote
Showed people honesty and truthfulness
Love of neighbour and faithfulness.
Christ implanted in our mind,
Ideas of service, a sacrificial kind.
This reservoir needs refilling
Not abandoning or rejecting.
"The way to personal flourishing
Is not by fiscal or social tinkering."

Culture of Celebrity

Do we live in a 'culture of celebrity'
Rather than one of 'personal integrity'?
Yes, we have exemplars, people of renown:
Entrepreneurs, medics, academic gown,
Nobel winners, scientific exploration,
Leaders of the British nation.
But there is the transient news in the media,
Entry in 'A-list', 'B-list' encyclopaedia;
'Big Brother', features in 'Hello' magazine;
Narcissistic need for attention, instant notoriety,
Story of the moment in a tabloid society.

Why do we give this fawning attention:
To Stars and idols this adulation?
Being in the public eye, the competition,
Even friends on Facebook show our position.
There's a craving to be a somebody
A longing for a 'cool' identity,
Desire for status or popularity.
Have we allowed the reservoirs to dry,
Drained older virtues without a 'why?'
Have we forgotten the idea of service,
Or finding oneself through self-sacrifice?[65]

I wrote the next poem in response to a young, bright and confident languages teacher who expressed confusion as to how she could relate her Christian faith to her professional practice as a teacher in a state school in England. Several readers have commented on its reverberation.

"Faith in the Work Place"

Should I consent to 'methodological agnosticism',
Confining my faith to the 'private' sphere,

---

[65] A winner in the Bedfordshire Libraries Poetry Competition 2012.

Keeping beliefs out of research and work, in a form
of 'dualism',
Bracketing-out my values, showing 'neutrality' that's
clear?

As teacher, Registrar, social worker, police officer or
nurse
Those paid out of the public purse,
Must we keep 'silent', to be inclusive,
Repress the unique claims of Christ as too exclusive?

Or can we bring those beliefs to our work that we
find inspiring
That motivate and drive our reason for being,
As we work out the application of 'The Great
Commission',
And the 'Great Commandment' with personal
conviction,

Lord help us to perceive how far we can go
The real extent of our freedom to know,
To be sensitive to our contractual demands,
But to follow faithfully our Lord's commands.

I can't be like Peter and just deny
My Christian faith when I need to say 'Why'.
Should I just be 'moral': action speaking louder than
word?
How can I relate faith to professional practice, not
just follow the herd?

There's not an inch of Creation
Not a particle, no system, no genetic variation,
No social or business transaction
Over which Jesus is not LORD. What declaration!

In conclusion, this chapter has looked generally at the
close relationship between poetry and prophecy. Then
briefly it surveyed the nature of prophecy in the Bible in
the Old and New Testaments. It illustrated how poetry
is related to prophecy and can be the medium of

prophecy. I have discussed views on prophecy today, and feel persuaded by Wayne Grudem's general thesis that prophecy is still meant to be operative in our Christian congregations (even with all the issues and problems of order, and validity it can bring [66]). We have God's final revelation in The Bible, which is our 'rule' of faith, but does that mean God no longer speaks through prophets, but exclusively through the Bible? Unlike my correspondent I feel that prophecy is not restricted now to powerful expository preaching.[67]

Erik Raymond commenting on his website [68]says: 'In the excellent book Preach the Word, D.A. Carson writes a most helpful chapter on "Challenges for the Twenty-first-century Pulpit." I quote in part below from a section where Carson is discussing what preaching actually is'.

"First preaching is more than the oral communication of information, no matter how biblical and divine that information may be. Rather, we should think in terms of what might be called 're-revelation.' …Preachers must bear this in mind. Their aim is more than to explain the Bible, however important that aim is. They want the proclamation of God's Word to be a revelatory event, a moment when God discloses himself afresh, a time when the people of God know that they have met with the living God." (Carson D.A. 2007).

---

[66] See Jay Gary discussing some of the issues 'Do You hear voices in your head? http://christianfutures.com/prophetic voices.shtml

[67] See the wise, modest and balanced video of John Piper speaking about Prophecy that supports this author's perspective.
http://pjcockrell.wordpress.com/2013/01/18/piper-on-tongues-and-prophecy/ (accessed January 16th, 2013)

[68] http://www.ordinarypastor.com/?p=1176 (accessed January 16th, 2013)

This author asks himself, 'Is it over-presumptuous to pray that poetry too (albeit in a lesser way) might be revelatory, a means of speaking to people, a channel for God's Spirit to comfort, to challenge and to build readers' faith?' I have concluded with Greg Haslam's wider interpretation of prophecy, that poetry can be the medium of communication through which God speaks to us about issues today. Poems can encourage, offer insight, re-reveal truth, and have a prophetic edge of speaking into socio/political situations. No doubt some readers may see this as didactic poetry, or apologetics. Of course, such revelation or prophecy must be evaluated by the teachings of the Bible to guard against false claims and deception into which we can all stray.

As children we used to sing Mary Maxwell's hymn 'How I praise Thee'. The language may seem dated, but this is still my prayer:

> Channels only, blessèd Master,
> But with all Thy wondrous power
> Flowing through us, Thou canst use us
> Every day and every hour[69]

[69] http://www.hymnary.org/hymn/TWC/577

References

Alter R. 1985 *The Art of Biblical Poetry*. New York: Basic Books Inc.

Asamoah-Gyadu K 2007. 'Prophecy', in the *Dictionary of Mission Theology*. Ed. Corrie J. Nottingham: IVP.

Bhagavad Gita http://www.bhagavad-gita.us/ (accessed 26/4/2011)

Brown C. 1978 *The New International Dictionary of Christian Theology*. Exeter: Paternoster

Carson D.A. 2007 Challenges for The 21st Century Pulpit. In Ryken L & Wilson T. 2007 *Preach The Word: Essays on Expository Preaching In Honour of R. Kent Hughes*. Wheaton. Illinois: Crossway Books.

Chard M. 2002. *Scribbling in The Sand. Christ and Creativity*. Leicester: IVP

Friebert S., Walker D., & Young D. Eds.1997 *A Field Guide To Contemporary Poetry and Poetics*. Oberlin: Ohio, US

Gabriel M. A. 2008 *Coffee With the Prophet*. Casselberry, Florida: Gabriel Publishing

Grudem W. 1994 *Systematic Theology*. Leicester: IVP

Grudem W. 1996 General Editor: 'Are Miraculous Gifts for Today?' Grand Rapids: Zondervan

Grudem W.A. 2000 *The Gift of Prophecy*. Wheaton, Illinois, US: Crossway

Guru Granth Sahib http://granthsahib.com/ (accessed 26/4/2011)

Haslam G. 2009. *Moving In The Prophetic*. Oxford: Monarch

http://www.biblegateway.com/passage/?search=Hosea%2014&version=NIV

http://www.hymnary.org/hymn/TWC/577

http://www.linkedin.com/pub/jackie-hill/19/758/741/

http://nobelprize.org/nobel_prizes/peace/laureates/1979/teresa-bio.html (accessed 27/4/2010)

http://martinlutherking.org/ (accessed 27/4/2011).

http://www.nelsonmandela.org/index.php (accessed 27/4/2011)

http://www.google.co.uk/#sclient=psy&hl=en&source=hp&q=poetic+inspiration&aq=0&aqi=g3g-v2&aql=&oq=&pbx=1&fp=495eca51a8ef0dd (accessed 27/4/2011)

http://jewishencyclopedia.com/view.jsp?artid=67&letter=P

http://christianfutures.com/prophetic-voices.shtml

http://en.wikipedia.org/wiki/Clairvoyance (accessed 27/4/2011)

http://en.wikipedia.org/wiki/Prophet

http://gbgm-umc.org/umhistory/wesley/hymns/ (accessed 4/7/2011)

Isaiah 40,1-2. New International Version. 1993. Cambridge: U of Cambridge

Jackman D. 2004. Let's Study 1 Corinthians. Edinburgh: Banner of Truth

Jewett P.K. 1974 Prophecy. *In The New Dictionary of The Christian Church* Ed. Douglas J.D. 1974. Exeter: Paternoster

Keene M. 1997. *Examining Four Religions*. Hong Kong: HarperCollins

Kendrick R. 1989. *Islam*. Oxford: Heinemann Educational

Kidner D. 1973 Poetry and Wisdom Literature. Introduction. In *The Lion Handbook to the Bible*. Alexander D. & Alexander P.1973. Berkhamsted: Lion Publishing

Kugel J.L. 1990 Ed. *Poetry and Prophecy*. New York: Cornell Univ. Press

Kugel J. 1981. *The Idea of Biblical Poetry*. London: John Hopkins Press

Levertof D. 1969. *Work and Inspiration: Inviting The Muse* in Friebert S, Walker D.

Motyer J.A. 1965. Prophecy. *The New Bible Dictionary*. Ed. Douglas J.D. London: IVF.

Prior D. 1985. *The Message of 1 Corinthians*. Nottingham: IVP.

The Daily Telegraph April 30th, 2011. p.6.7, and 19. London: Telegraph Media Group

The Dalai Lama. (Tenzin Gyatso)2007. *Mind in Comfort and Ease*. Somerville. USA: Wisdom Pub.

Tutu D. 2004. *God Has A Dream*. London: Rider (Imprint of Ebury Press).

Webb D. 2007 *Animal Painting Workbook*. Cincinnati, US: David & Charles

Wheeler Robinson H. 1956 *The Religious Ideas of The Old Testament*. London: Duckworth.

Young D. 1997 A *Field Guide To Contemporary Poetry and Poetics*. Ohio, US: Oberlin

Yousef M.H. 2011. *Son of Hamas*. Milton Keynes: Authentic Media

Zayid M.Y.1980 *The Qur'an*. Beirut, Lebanon: Dar Al-Chora

Questions for Reflection:

1. How are the words 'prophet' and 'prophecy' used in speech?

2. How are prophets in the Old Testament distinctive?

3. What were the purposes of prophecy in the New Testament?

4. Explain three interpretations of the use of prophecy in the Church in our time.

5. To what extent do you agree with the author's views about the connection between poetry and prophecy?

6. In what sense might a poem have a 'prophetic dimension', or 'speak to people'?

7. Which poem did you enjoy or find helpful?

CHAPTER 4

POETRY as THEOLOGICAL REFLECTION

"the Lord has need of you"

Water colour painting by the author

Palm Sunday

We needed political action,
Independence, liberation,
Freedom from foreign forces:
Occupation's expulsion.
We've dreamed of deliverers
Messiah's and saviours.

When He rode into the Capital
We thought it strategically vital
He brought weapons for arming
His followers that morning,
But a 'donkey', an ass,
With an excitable mass!

They praised Him that Sunday,
Branches waved by the way,
'Save now, Oh Lord',
As promised by prophetic word.
But, the 'King' came in humility
And wept for our doomed city.

Some failed to recognise
And would later despise
The Servant of the Lord's suffering,
His sacrifice and offering.
Meanwhile, moneychangers were dispersed,
And the national 'Fig-tree' cursed.

Our religious leaders schemed
(Through fear and envy it seemed),
To suppress, arrest, and disown
His royal kingdom and throne.
Jesus, the doomed city lamenting,
His redeemed people was saving.

In this chapter, I explore the writing of poetry as a 'means' and as a 'product' of theological reflection. Firstly, I trace the impact that Christian poetry had on the development of my faith and understanding of Christianity in early years. Many of my poems are reflections about faith issues. I give examples of using poetry to meditate on scripture, and to internalize the truth I have heard expressed in preaching. I discuss what we might mean by 'theological reflection', describing two practical methods of using poetry for this purpose. Then I give examples of poems that illustrate the process of reflecting theologically.

Some of my earliest memories of my religious education are my mother's prayers at the bedside. I can still picture the devotion of my parents, their kneeling in prayer, and their regular reading of their old leather-bound Bibles. They loved the songs and hymns that we played on the record player on Sundays after lunch. In childhood, religious songs from CSSM Choruses[1], and hymns helped stimulate my thinking about God, Jesus, and the sacred text. Hymns, particularly the poems of Charles Wesley[2] and Frances Ridley Havergal[3] were influential in nurturing faith. The words of hymns and songs brought encouragement at stressful times. My mother recited poems about the life of faith at Church celebrations.

As a teenager, I learned to sing the bass lines to hymns with a group around a piano at a Fellowship Club on Saturday evenings. Poems about faith, the product of authors' theological reflection, helped develop my beliefs. They were a kind of embryonic theology in poetry and song.

In later life (when great hymns have been neglected by some sections of the Church), I have come to appreciate the language, verse forms, and deep spiritual reflection of hymn writers of earlier generations. F.W.Faber's 'My God, how wonderful thou art'[4] inspires awe and personal devotion in worship. His 'Souls of Men, why will ye scatter'[5] has been a source of spiritual encouragement. There are memorable phrases that echo down through two centuries: 'There's a wideness in God's mercy'; 'For the love of God is broader than the measures of man's mind'. George Herbert's poems from two hundred years' earlier still reverberate with

---

[1] CSSM Choruses 2 http://www.amazon.co.uk/Choruses-Childrens-Special-Service-Mission/dp/B0010XS19S/rcf=sr_1_3?s=books&ie=UTF8&qid=1325177139&sr=1-3 (accessed 29 Dec 2011)
[2] See helpful article and list of hymns: http://en.wikipedia.org/wiki/Charles_Wesley (accessed 29 Dec 2011)
[3] *The Ministry of Song*. 1885. London: James Nisbet & Co.
[4] P.219 *Hymns Ancient and Modern*. 1988. *Hymns Ancient and Modern Ltd*. Beccles, Suffolk.
[5] P.555. *Hymns Ancient and Modern*. Op.cit. above.

insight and inspiration: 'Let all the world in every corner sing…', and 'Teach me my God and king…'[6]

Every culture will have its own 'Songs of Zion' that need transmitting to the next generation. In the UK, while we rejoice in the fresh new inspirational songs of Timothy Dudley Smith[7] ,Graham Kendrick[8], Noel and Tricia Richards[9], and Stuart Townsend's Live Worship from Ireland: 'Hear the call of the kingdom.'[10], our children will be denied their spiritual heritage of song and poetry if we do not teach them the hymns of Isaac Watts ('Joy to the world, the Lord has come!'), Bernard of Cluny ('Jerusalem the Golden'), H. Bonar ('Here O my Lord may I behold your face', William Rees ('Here is love, vast as the ocean').

As I have commented, many of my own poems are reflections about faith issues: meditations, responses of the mind and emotions to reading or to sermons, or about relating my faith to life. On occasions as I listen to sermons, I write what I am hearing in verse. This can be an aid to listening and digesting of the content, or it can be a response to the sermon. Sometimes I go home, and research the topic more systematically and then compress the ideas in a poem. On other occasions, I summarize what I have been thinking about in the form of a poem.

The meditative process is valuable. There is a discipline involved in writing about your thoughts. Writing also aids 'active listening' to sermons, in

[6] P.449, and p. 531 *Hymns Ancient & Modern*. Op.cit.
[7] Behold a Broken World… Hymn 949. Praise. 2000. Darlington: Praise Trust.
[8] Oh Lord, the clouds are gathering…'. Hymn 953. 'Beauty for brokenness, hope for despair…'. Hymn 944. Praise. 2000. Darlington: Praise Trust'
[9] 'Our Confidence is in the Lord…'. Hymn 786. Praise. Op.cit.
[10] Compact disc: KMDC2826. There is A Hope. Townsend S. 2008. Eastbourne: Kingsway Music.

replicating the ideas, interpreting and evaluating, and applying the message. This is in the spirit of Luke's comment about the Berean Christians being 'more noble than those at Thessalonica'.[11]

In some meditations, I write out portions from the Bible as poems. I find the reading, the understanding of the text, and the writing within a structure hard work, but a helpful form of meditation. Some poems like this take several weeks to write. Here is an extract of the meditation written on the letter of James. The poetic structure is less important than the process of meditation:

James 1, 9-16

Kingdom ethics
Turn ideas on their head:
"The rich" can be 'poor' instead,
"A high position",
Can be a low condition.
The rich can pass away
Like a day lily withering:
It's beauty here today,
But quickly fading.
Happy the man who remains faithful
Experiencing trials. He is successful
In passing such a test.
He will receive a reward: God's Rest.
But when tempted and trialled
We should not be beguiled.
God from evil is exempt,
And will no one tempt.
We yield to our desiring,
To trapping and drawing,
Conceiving our sinning,
So avoid this deceiving.
The prevalent evil disrupting.

---

[11] Acts 17,11

The Word which was planted
Needs to be humbly accepted,
Not merely listening,
But doing what it's saying.
It's so easy to glance quickly
In the mirror and go away,
Forgetting our image
For the rest of the day.

Rob Wynalda's 'The 17:18 Series' provided me with a way of reflection on the Bible. These books are designed so that on one page you write out scripture long-hand, and on the opposite page you write comments. I chose to write the passage as poetic verse instead.

Wynalda explains:

'The Journible is a profoundly simple attempt to aid a person's ability to engage the Word of God by slowing down the process of simply reading the text'. 'In Deuteronomy 17, the king is told to hand-write his own copy of the law'.

Wynalda says that its purpose was so that the king would read it, learn to fear the Lord, obey the commands of God, that his heart would not become proud, that he would not turn to the right or left, and that his sons would serve after him.[12] I have found this process of writing a demanding but beneficial way of meditating on the text.

Here is another meditation, this time on the Lord's Prayer that attempts to draw-out the meaning of the text:

Our Father:

Creator,
Originator,

---

[12] See p.5. The 17: 18 Series: James, 1 Peter, 2 Peter, 1 John, 2 John, 3 John, Jude. Wynalda R. 2009. Grand Rapids: Reformation Heritage Books

Designer, Sustainer;
'Image' imparter,
Provider, protector;
Trinity and unity,
With Spirit and Son
The loving Holy One.

Who art in Heaven:
God's dwelling place
'Above', 'Beyond', 'other' than
Material: time and space.
Yet from each of us not far away,
When we draw near to Him and pray.

Hallowed be Thy Name:
The resplendent glory,
The full story
Shrouded in His name,
He will not give to another:
'Yahweh'. His fame:
"I am" and "will be"
Lord Most High.
One day we'll see.
Now with awe and reverence
We come with penitence,
In faith and love bowing
His great name hallowing.

Thy Kingdom come
Thy will be done on Earth as it is in Heaven:
'Basileia', kingly rule and government:
Not a vision of social improvement;
Not a present reality solely,
Nor a future event exclusively.
God breaking through,
The 'now' but 'not yet'.
Messianic promises were met,
But there's a future fulfilment too!
Lord, human society, the whole Creation
Groans with longing expectation

For your will to be done on Earth:
Bring justice, and shalom to birth
Through our actions and responsibility,
Then through your purposes for all Eternity.

Give us this day our daily bread:
Lord we take so much for granted
The plenty that others have planted.
Forgive us that in our haste
There is food that we waste.
Thank you that You have said
"You are the Living Bread".
"This is My body, take and eat",
Communion as together we meet.
We labour for bread that will perish
Forgetting food we should cherish.

And forgive us our trespasses
As we forgive those who have
Trespassed against us
Forgiveness:
'Lifting',
'Carrying',
'Bearing',
'Graciously dealing',
'Sending away', 'loosing'.
God is merciful, gracious
Long suffering,
Abundant in goodness
And truth,
Mercy keeping
For thousands,
Iniquity forgiving,
Transgressions blotting,
Guilt and sin pardoning.
A sacrifice atoning
For the penitent confessing,
Wrath assuaging
At the mercy seat propitiating:

Jesus our ransom, redeeming,
His death substituting
Representing and justifying
To God reconciling.
The Father initiating,
The Son accomplishing,
The Spirit convicting,
Remission applying,
As we too are forgiving
Of those who are offending,
Against us who are sinning.

And lead us not into temptation
But deliver us from evil
Lord, do not bring me to hard testing.
I am tempted by my evil desiring,
Pride and appetites conspiring.
You test our genuineness, our loyalty
To strengthen our maturity,
But Satan seeks to seduce and destroy
Disgracing with strategies he'll employ.
Lord, deliver me from the Evil One.
Give me strength to overcome.

For Thine is the kingdom
The power
And the glory
For ever and ever
Amen.

This 17:18 process makes the writer wrestle with the questions:

What does the text say?

What does it mean?

What implications are there for me today?

It seems Puritan writers composed similar poems on Bible texts and beliefs.[13] Poems provide a space, and a discipline in which theological reflection may take place. Writing can be both a process and a product of this thinking. Thus, the composition is a creative form of theological reflection, and the poem itself can be shared with friends as product of reflection. I have received positive feedback on both the method of meditation on the Lord's Prayer, and appreciative comments about the content, the product of the poem.

What can we say about theological reflection, or reflecting theologically?[14] At its simplest level it can be meditating on a passage from the Bible at home, or discussing it in a group study. It can be addressing questions about faith and life in a house group. At a profounder level, it can be deeper thought about theological topics or issues based on study.

'theological reflection is learning how to reflect on the action of God in our lives and the life of the Christian community. Reflection is something we do all the time; when we think about the meaning or significance of a book or movie or an event, we are reflecting. In theological reflection we use Scripture, Church teaching, sacramental events and contemporary life as the basis for our reflection. The most common example of theological reflection is the Sunday homily. The preacher uses Scripture as a

---

[13] See http://www.puritansermons.com/poetry/taylor.htm and http://www.facebook.com/pages/Puritan-and-Reformed-Poetry/128439560537606 See http://en.wikipedia.org/wiki/Meditative_poetry (accessed October 4th, 2012).

[14] See Susanna Snyder's review of *Theological Reflection Methods* by Elaine Graham, Heather Wilson, and Frances Ward. London: SCM Press, 2005. http://www.practicalmattersjournal.org/issue/3/reviews/the ological-reflection

foundation to talk about its meaning in our own lives and the life of the Church and world. In a theological reflection exercise you become the homilist, relating some aspect of Church teaching to your daily life in a way that helps you learn more about God and God's presence and action in your life'.[15]

Abigail Johnson's article fits well with my experience when she says that theological reflection is simply wondering about God's activity in our lives. It is asking questions like 'Where is God present?', 'What is God calling us to do?' By taking time to ask questions about the nature of God, God's purposes, and his revelation in the Bible we are reflecting theologically. By questioning what happens to us and by seeing our experiences through the lens of faith we can develop our faith and become clearer about our relationship to God. It is a normal human activity to ask questions, or to ponder about relationships, our work, our children, our government, and our situation in life. We all reflect, wonder, analyze, think, assess, and discuss with friends as ways of trying to understand our life. Theological reflection simply refocuses all that thinking to encourage a stronger sense of our relationship with God, asking, "Where does God fit into the picture?" [16] [17]

In reading about 'theological reflection' I was

---

[15] The Skill of Theological Reflection from
http://eps.trinitydc.edu/Theological_Reflection.doc
(accessed 16/6/2011)
[16] See Abigail Johnson of 'Alban': Theological Reflection in a Small Group.
http://www.alban.org/conversation.aspx?id=2674
(accessed 16/6/2011)
[17] Reflecting with God: Connecting Faith and Daily Life in Small Groups 2004 Alban Institute

attracted to E.F.M.s (Education for Ministry)[18] four phases of identifying, exploring, connecting, and applying because they echoed the action–research cycle with which I am familiar,[19] and the notion of the 'reflective practitioner'[20] which has had a deep influence on my professional life in education.

The first step is identifying the subject, issue or question to consider, whether it is a life experience, a belief, an aspect of the Christian tradition, or text from the Bible, or a theme from contemporary culture.

The second phase explores that subject, using a series of questions designed to enquire, explore and stimulate thoughts and feelings.

The third phase is the making connections with wider sources of meaning and truth. It asks questions about how the exploration of the selected subject fits in with Christian beliefs, our life, and society. Some of the questions considered in both phases two and three are "perspective questions" that encourage us to get inside the subject and view things from a different perspective. An example is "What kind of a world do we find here?" As the process moves along, all four sources of understanding are brought in.

The last phase of the reflection, considers what insights and implications there are for action that have been found during the process. For E.F.M. it is a group activity, but for the poet it can also be singular and individual, then shared with community.

The author's poems that might be termed 'theological reflection' were written for various

---

[18] See:
http://www.efm.org.nz/reflections/methods_of_tr.htm (accessed 16/6/2011)
[19] See *Educational Action Research. An International Journal.* Abingdon: Taylor and Francis
[20] See http://en.wikipedia.org/wiki/Reflective_practice for reflection applied to professional practice in education and health care. (Accessed 16/6/2011)

audiences. Some were personal to concentrate on the preacher's message, or to clarify or express his own thinking. Others were written for individuals to encourage faith, proclaim Christian beliefs, or to inform. Then I have made some available on web sites and blogs for a wider audience,[21] including the poem 'Heaven'. It was written during some thoughtful reading about the subject at a time of ill health. It expresses my faith, and joyful anticipation of Heaven, and the New Creation. It made the thought of dying less depressing. I have had positive comments from readers, saying that they found it helpful and encouraging.

Heaven
Christians often talk about
Heaven, ('for ever with the Lord' living),
But in fact the Biblical teaching
Is richer than this, beyond doubt.
"Then", said the Seer, "I saw",
(And we bow with joy and awe),
"A new heaven and Earth"
That had come to birth.
The first heaven and earth
Had passed away.
They disappeared with a roaring.
The elements with heat melting,
As Peter said in his writing.
The heavens will be new (or renewed,
Depending on how the text is viewed),

---

[21] See e.g. http://transformingresearch.ning.com/
http://bwakeman.wordpress.com/   (accessed 16/6/2011)
http://www.christianpoetry.org/selentry-3.php?aid=3140
(site now closed in 2012)
http://www.actforhim.org.uk/resources/Am_I_Listening.pdf
(accessed 16/6/2011)
http://allpoetry.com/poem/7263786-
The_Time_for_Salvation_Is_Now-by-MJ_Donnelly
(accessed 16/6/2011)

And the Earth too we are told
The home of peace and righteousness
As Isaiah had foretold,
Free from pain and distress.
The Creation will be set free
From its bondage and decay.
We anticipate glorious liberty
In bodies of the resurrection
To serve in a fulfilling way.
We will inherit the Earth
And reign as God's original intention.
This is not expressed mythologically,
But a real hope theologically.
There's physical eating.
With Jesus we'll be drinking.
'The Water of Life', some symbols, yes:
'The Tree with its fruit';
'A Holy City', nonetheless.
Peeps into a new reality,
Perhaps with technology and creativity?
God dwelling with men
Who've laid up treasure in heaven.
There'll be ruling and reigning,
The presence on Earth of His Glory,
Beauty and joy, no pain or dying,
No mourning or crying.
This life is a preparation,
A process of training
For future ruling and reigning.
What a hope for proclamation!

"To Die is Gain" is a similar meditation, but on the 'in-between' state, between death and the Second Coming of Christ. Even though people may need some clarity and reassurance on this issue, is it not rather odd that I have heard very few sermons on the nature of the after-life?

Here I raise questions (as in the E.F.M. model for reflection mentioned earlier). Then I draw on 'connections with wider sources of meaning and truth' as suggested with two perspectives on heaven for the Christian believer. There is some speculation about consciousness after death, and then reference to the Bible on the Second Coming of Jesus, the Resurrection and New Heavens and Earth. The last phase of the reflection, (considering what 'insights and implications there are for action that have been found during the process') is the effect on the writer, and any receptive reader. For me it strengthened faith and hope. The author invites the reader to respond to the poem.

"To Die is Gain"

When we take our last
Our final faltering breath,
When our eyes close in death
And our time here is past,
Will we sink into a soul-sleep
Unconscious, a disembodied spirit?
Or will we be awake, aware,
Enjoying a 'dwelling place' we inherit:
'Paradise', promised, beyond compare,
To the thief who was penitent
That Jesus said He would prepare?
"With Christ" better to greater extent
Than all the joys, the wonders here:
For no eye has seen, no ear
Has heard, mind conceived
What God has prepared
For those who love Him.
Perhaps in His presence aware in a way
Of life on Earth as the 'witness cloud',
Able to worship and to pray
"Oh Sovereign Lord" With voices loud
"Salvation belongs to God" enthroned,
Conscious fellowship with God in Heaven

"Praise to the Lamb" who atoned.
For His Second Coming we'll be waiting,
Changed in 'the twinkling of an eye',
New resurrection bodies anticipating.
For this mortal must become 'immortal',
This perishable put on the 'incorruptible'.
Meanwhile the whole of Creation
Yearns for this revelation!

The next poem 'Mind the Gap' was developed in preparation for a research seminar at OCMS,[22] Oxford. I based it on thinking that had taken place over several months. An imaginary conversation is developed between a Christian and Jesus that explores the false dualism between the sacred and secular that can creep into church teaching unintentionally. Our secular work can be relegated as secondary, less important than 'church activities', (of worship services, listening to preaching, evangelism, and so-called 'spiritual' activities). Yet we spend most of our time in normal everyday activities like work, leisure, and family life. Has the gospel 'to the whole of creation' nothing to say about our lives in the secular World (other than the strong ethical implications of faith)?

Mind The Gap

Mind The Gap…
Between the 'theory' and the 'action',
The 'claims' and the 'concrete',
Between 'Profession' and 'Practice',
'Sunday' and 'Monday' service,
Eschewing a false dualism
Between the 'sacred' and 'secular'.

Lord, I walk up the stairs
Into corporate expectations,

---

[22] Oxford Centre for Mission Studies.

A different set of values.
I become intensely immersed
Into Company considerations,
So easily crowding out You.

Son, Think about the Big Story.
I am Creator and Redeemer.
You are made in My image.
'Redeem' your work creatively
With all My excellency,
With a servant heart.

Lord, How do I redeem my work?
So much is repetitive and routine.
How can I relate my Christian values
Legitimately to the work place
Closing the yawning space
Between 'private' and 'public'?

Daughter, 'Working' is part of My 'image'.
In what you do, see it is 'good'.
Be creative and energetic,
Faithful and trustworthy.
You make a witness in a way
By what you 'do' and what you 'say'.

In providing a home and food,
In working for family's good,
In using your talent and skill,
In contributing to the culture
You are 'having dominion'
Serving and doing My will.

Some pastors or ministers may see potential harm in members of the congregation writing about a sermon in verse, as one commented:

"when you write a poem based on a sermon, you put the prophetic ministry of the preacher's exposition through the filter of your mind and re-issue it, and it is this which is potentially problematic to the preacher if the poem appears in the public domain as a published work (particularly if you identify the name of the preacher and the church), as it potentially adjusts or revises the message we have preached"[23]

As a direct response, I have removed references to names and venues when responding to sermons with poems. I still maintain that the deep reflection involved in writing helps me internalise the sermon, and makes available the ideas to a wider audience. Comments I have received from readers by e-mail indicate that some poems help readers to understand the preaching, and they develop further ideas and insights.

The insights of sermons, the product of hours of thought, prayer and energy in preparation, can so easily be forgotten by listeners. How can congregations take the message to heart, apply it, and grow in faith and the knowledge of God? Writing the ideas in verse is one way of meditating, internalising and applying the message so it reverberates through the congregation. Of course we must beware of allowing our focus to be distracted from the possibility of 'listening to God' by concentration on writing the poem itself.

Another form of theological reflection is meditating about the content of the books we are reading. A poem can capture the central ideas. On reading the books 'Beyond Homelessness', and 'Hope in Troubled Times',[24] (and in relating my understanding to Christian action-research), I wrote 'Hope':

---

[23] Private e-mail

[24] *Beyond Homelessness, Christian Faith in a Culture of Displacement*. Bouma-Prediger S., Walsh .J. 2008. Grand Rapids, Michigan: Eerdmans

Hope in Troubled Times. Goodzward B., Vander Vennen M., Van Heemst D, 2007. Grand Rapids, Michigan: Baker Academic

Hope

Is there just cold, blind indifference
To our questions and striving
For meaning and coherence,
Any answers mere contriving?

Hope is the confident expectation
Of a future good in imagination,
Looking for the real possibility,
Longing for the coming reality.
Imagination, faith and desire
Combined in a vision to inspire.

In research there may be some distortion,
Efforts misdirected, want of proportion,
And some actions remain unimplemented,
Focus changes before plans are cemented.
Hope drives us on to endeavour again:
No submission, "It's not in vain".

I am required to 'love justice, do mercy',
Renew my mind, work righteously,
Improve my service, do good to all,
Reverse the corroding effects of the Fall,
Strive for His will to be done on Earth
Now and in the future World's rebirth.

The next poem is a meditation on reading 'The Cross of Christ' by John Stott.[25] Each Easter I try to read something that refreshes and deepens my understanding of the meaning of the passion narratives. I find John Stott's writing informative and inspirational. This is a book about which Howard Marshall is reported to have said, "This could well be the most important evangelical book on the cross since James Denney."

The revered Evangelical leader, John Stott said:

"I try to show that the cross transforms everything. It gives us a new, worshipping relationship to God, a

[25] *The Cross of Christ*. John Stott 1989. Leicester: IVP

new and balanced understanding of ourselves, a new incentive to give ourselves in mission, a new love for our enemies, and a new courage to face the perplexities of suffering."[26]

The Cross is Crucial

Just why then did Christ die?
Judas delivered Him to Priests,
Then Pilate to Herod.
Soldiers killed Him. (Is that why?)
But, the Father 'Gave Him up'.
Jesus gave Himself willingly.
Look at His words carefully
In Upper Room, in the Garden,
In Cry of Dereliction for our pardon.
Surely it relates to our sin?
The problem of forgiveness:
The conflict between
The majesty of God (is seen)
And the gravity of our sin;
His holiness, justice and His love
To satisfy Himself (the sinner to win)
He substituted Himself
In Christ the Saviour for us.
The Cross has achieved
Salvation for sinners (who believed),
The Revelation of God
And the conquest of evil,
Propitiation, Redemption,
Justification and Reconciliation!

The next poem was composed for a research student enquiring into 'moral competence'. It draws upon my research for writing a book,[27] some studying for a higher degree, and on reflection since. It shows a compression

---

[26] P.11 in the Preface. *The Cross of Christ*.
[27] Wakeman B.E. 1984. *Personal Social and Moral Education*. Tring: Lion

of thinking, and a density of ideas within a space provided by the poem's structure. The form is somewhat clumsy, but the poem illustrates theological reflection at a deeper level. It addresses the question: 'What is moral competence for the Christian?' (that was, the student's focus of interest).

It is not arid academic theological reflection, but has practical application to professional ethics in education, nursing, and social work. It is a form of Practical Theology.[28] The professional teacher, counsellor, or mentor wrestles with what moral competence means for them and for their clients. Philosophical presuppositions about ethics, 'oughts' and a vision of the good life, are embedded in professional practice. Expectations at work can clash with Christian beliefs. The Christian needs to think hard about how far they should, and can, express their faith in the public, secular world. As Paul said, "work out your salvation with fear and trembling". This poem had a particular group in mind that was able to think about the ideas expressed, rather than for a wider, general audience.

Moral Competence?

We come with our cultivated goodness, pride and
  moral autonomy,
In our carefully clarified, prized and acted values
  economy,
Notions of right and wrong: my existential choices,
Intuitive grasp of good and evil voices,
Moral philosophy and competent moral thinking,
With my grasp of higher levels of justice reasoning,
Even with my finer feelings, empathy,
Respect for persons, consideration, sympathy,
My political correctness, and the social forms
Of acceptable behaviour, cultural norms…

---

[28] For a succinct description, see
http://en.wikipedia.org/wiki/Practical_theology (accessed 25th November 2012.

In Romans, I read that I fall short of God's glory,
No one righteous in God's sight: that's the story.
"All we like sheep have gone astray,
We have turned everyone to his own way".
In the glare of holy, burning transcendent light
No high-born, or devotee can claim the 'moral right'.
This is where Christian morality begins,
Like the prophet Isaiah with a consciousness of sins:
Holy, holy is the Lord God Almighty.
The whole Earth is full of his glory.
Woe to me, I am ruined, a man of unclean lips
And I live in a tainted society.

So have I inherited a total 'ethical depravity'?
With such a notion I've never been happy.
Do I not have conscience as a guide, an 'inner light'?
Are there not vestiges of goodness or moral insight?
What of acts of kindness without reciprocity we
    personally require,
Or of justice, or of human virtues: love, and
    forgiveness we admire?
The nurture in families, and for protection: society's
    laws?
Surely moral action reflects the Divine Image
    whatever the flaws?
Moral reprobation or incompetence is not the
    Scriptures' import
But that my highest thoughts or deeds of God's
    standards fall short.

We may find stage theories, or discover moral
    reasoning skills.
Greater or lesser competence for coping with
    behavioural ills.
Degrees of self-actualisation, living at peace with self
    and the other,
Harmony with nature, 'principles to live by', we may
    discover.

> So, what is distinctively Christian, of what 'moral'
> development do we speak?
> What is 'moral competence', what 'fruit' of
> redemption should we seek?
> 'Faith and love springing', 'bearing fruit' and
> 'growing' metaphors from Paul,
> A relational morality: 'pleasing Him'; 'doing all in His
> name', clear advice for us all:
> 'Put to death malice and slander', 'with compassion
> and kindness clothe yourself'.
> Here are some signposts to degrees of moral
> competence and health.

I use poetic forms of writing to explore issues of practical theology.[29] In this next poem, I am applying key Biblical concepts to the situation in which many Christian teachers find themselves. The poem was written by request for ACT[30] to encourage teachers to apply their faith to professional practice in what can seem a lonely and hostile secular environment.

Together we are stronger

> Singly, we can feel alone,
> Isolated on our own,
> Faith subject to suppression,
> Mild forms of persecution.
> Our impartiality,
> Correctness politically
> Squeeze us into a mould

---

[29]See e.g. http://www.gotquestions.org/practical-thcology.html (accessed July 2nd, 2011)
And for further references:
http://www.amazon.co.uk/s/?ie=UTF8&keywords=practical+theology&tag=yahhyd-21&index=stripbooks&hvadid=37255573031&ref=pd_sl_5l9s4teevj_b   (both accessed 29/12/2011)
[30] ACT. The Association of Christian Teachers.
http://www.christian-teachers.org.uk/ (accessed 29/12/2011)

Where faith we are told
"Is for the private sphere
Not for the 'public' here."

But truth, beauty and goodness
Education must address.
Faith's not in opposition
Rather, our motivation:
'Chesed' our loving-kindness,
'Shalom' concern for wholeness.[31]
'Pistos' and 'aletheia'[32]
Make it abundantly clear
Our high estimate of truth
For our children and youth.

Singly we are frail strands,
But together in God's hands
We can be a rescue cable,
Chain links that are able
To withstand opposition,
Bricks in a supporting position,
Chalk with colour and texture
Adding to the vivid picture
Of human education
By skills and dedication.

In his article "Theological Method", R. Lints says that theology is not simply a list of dogmas to be believed:

"but encompasses a framework for thinking about God and God's world and a vision for living in it. Theology must be lived in the life of the church and also lived in the midst of the world. As a result, it is a study of enormously complex and complicated dimensions... Theology that is distinctively Christian

---

[31] Hebrew words

[32] Greek for faith, faithfulness, truth and truthfulness

is not primarily human reflection on the meaning of life. It is centrally about listening to a divine word"[33]

So 'theological reflection' can be 'enormously complex' as any library of theology demonstrates. However, it is not just an intellectual process. The application, the working out of faith in social settings is vital. Lints goes further commenting later in his article:

"Finally, theology ought to be framed within the context of doxology. Reflections upon God should be wrapped in praise and adoration of God. The entire theological endeavour must be understood in the context of knowing and worshiping God. Theology ought not only to serve our minds… but must also be grounded in a heart prepared by God"[34]

The next poem echoes the idea of theological reflection being framed within the context of doxology.

The Trinity

To understand the Trinity
The mysteries of Divinity?
Athanasius saw the need
To exclude errors with his Creed.
It was impossible to define
Christ's natures 'human' and 'Divine'!
But 'hypostaseis' rules Arians out of court
'Homoousios' was what Nicaea had taught.

We can faintly grasp the roles and relationship:
Father, Son, and Spirit in perfect fellowship.
Mystery too complex for theologians' sagacity
Far beyond mere human capacity!
"Three persons in one Divine Essence."
Stand in awe and worship in His presence!

---

[33] In *New Dictionary of Christian Apologetics*
[34] p.705. *Theological Reflection.*

In this chapter, I have discussed the use of poetry as a process of reflection about sermons, and the writing of the content of scripture as verse. I outlined E.F.M's approach to theological reflection, and have given examples of meditations and theological reflection in and through poetry. I do not want to make exaggerated claims, or make too a strong a case, but I do believe reflection through the discipline and creativity of poetry deserves a place alongside the more traditional forms of private meditation on scripture, and public exposition of texts. It deserves creative space alongside academic reflection in theological essays, systematic and practical theologies, and lectures, seminars, and discussion groups. Moreover, we need fresh poems, songs and hymns to express our faith, and to give glory to God in worship. I invite readers to try out some of the ideas and verse forms mentioned in this chapter in their own theological reflection, and worship.

References

ACT. The Association of Christian Teachers. http://www.christian-teachers.org.uk/

Bouma-Prediger S. and Walsh J. 2008. *Beyond Homelessness, Christian Faith in a Culture of Displacement…* Grand Rapids, Michigan: Eerdmans

Campbell-Jack C., & McGrath G.J. 2006. eds. *New Dictionary of Apologetics.* Leicester: IVP.

Goodzward B., Vander Vennen M., Van Heemst D, 2007. *Hope in Troubled Times.* Grand Rapids, Michigan: Baker Academic

Graham E., Wilson H., Ward F., 2005. *Theological Reflection Methods* London: SCM Press

http://www.practicalmattersjournal.org/issue/3/reviews/theological-reflection (accessed 16/6/2011)

Johnson A. Theological Reflection in a Small Group http://www.alban.org/conversation.aspx?id=2674 (accessed 16/6/2011)

Johnson A. 2005 R*eflecting with God*: *Connecting Faith and Daily Life in Small Groups.* Atlanta US: The Alban Institute

http://www.efm.org.nz/reflections/methods_of_tr.htm (accessed 16/6/2011)

http://transformingresearch.ning.com/ (accessed 22/7/2011)

http://bwakeman.wordpress.com/ accessed 22/7/2011

http://www.christianpoetry.org/selentry-3.php?aid−3140 accessed 22/7/2011 http://www.actforhim.org.uk/resources/Am_I_Listening.pdf (accessed 20/7/2011)

http://allpoetry.com/poem/7263786-The_Time_for_Salvation_Is_Now-by-MJ_Donnelly (accessed 6/7/2011)

http://en.wikipedia.org/wiki/Reflective_practice (accessed 22/7/2011)

Hymns Ancient & Modern New Standard. 1988. Beccles: Hymns Ancient & Modern Ltd.

Praise. 2000. Darlington: Praise Trust.

Stott J. 1989. *The Cross of Christ.* John Stott 1989. Leicester: IVP

Wynalda R. 2009. The 17: 18 Series: James, 1 Peter, 2 Peter, 1 John, 2 John, 3 John, Jude. Grand Rapids. Michigan: Reformation Heritage Books

Questions for Reflection:

"All we like sheep have gone astray.
We have turned every one to his own way…"
Isaiah 53,6.
Photo: The author

What is theological reflection?

Describe one method the author discusses.

Which poem illustrates theological reflection most vividly for you?

What could you do in your meditations to introduce some theological reflection in poetic forms?

CHAPTER 5

POETRY as WISDOM

Wisdom in Poetry?

Can a mere stanza or verse
Compactly composed, or terse
Bring comfort, consolation,
Challenge or admonition?
Is there disclosure, learning,
Ideas or insights revealing
Reflecting on imagery
Metaphor or simile?
Can poetry have wisdom
For blessing in God's Kingdom?

Another way of looking at poetry from a Christian perspective is seeing some verse standing in the tradition of the genre of Wisdom literature of the Bible. 'Wisdom' is a fruitful category for interpreting some forms of poetry. Poetry as wisdom can avoid the uneasiness an author may feel about associating poetry with prophecy. Poetry paired with prophecy can feel presumptuous, even when discussed in a broad and lower sense of encouragement, consolation and challenge as in my previous chapter Poetry and Prophecy.

'Wisdom' in common speech is prudence, showing careful thought about consequences. It is shown in balanced judgement, in being skilful or well informed. We ask, 'Is that wise?' meaning 'Is it sensible'? Wise choices are made after due consideration, weighing the best advice we can get, and thinking about possible consequences. The dictionary definition[1] is "the quality of being wise"; "the body of knowledge and experience that develops within a specified society or period". To be wise is 'having or showing experience, knowledge, and good judgement'. It is being aware, and knowing how to act.

There is a wisdom of tribal elders,[2] of an elderly farmer, or of a senior accountant who have developed deep knowledge, understanding and skill of their field. Younger managers may make hasty dynamic decisions, whereas wiser leaders draw on their accumulated knowledge and skill, of similar cases which they bring to bear on present situations. Wisdom can lie in professional practice where lawyers, doctors, or teachers reflect about their work, drawing on accumulated understanding, experience and competence which they relate to present cases.

It is interesting that one dictionary[3] that is usually illuminating in its articles about modern thought has no entry under 'wisdom' or 'wise'. There is more help in *The Cambridge Dictionary of Philosophy*.[4]

"an understanding of the highest principles of things that functions as a guide for living a truly exemplary human life... Aristotle introduced a distinction between theoretical wisdom (sophia) and practical wisdom (phronesis) the former being the intellectual

[1] *Concise Oxford English Dictionary*. Ed. Soanes C. & Stevenson A. 2009. Eleventh Edition, Revised. Oxford: OUP.
[2] See wisdom of healing plants:
http://nopr.niscair.res.in/bitstream/123456789/9775/1/IJT K%209%283%29%20467-470.pdf (accessed October 4th, 2012)
Wisdom of Eskimo elder: see:
http://www.knewways.com/2009/04/wisdom-from-eskimo-kalaallit-elder-angaangaq/ (accessed October 4th, 2012).
[3] *New Fontana Dictionary of Modern Thought*. Ed. Bullock A, & Trombley S. 2000. London: HarperCollins
[4] Ed. Audi R. 2001. Cambridge: Cambridge University Press

virtue that disposed one to grasp the nature of reality in terms of its ultimate causes (metaphysics), the latter being the ultimate practical virtue that disposed one to make sound judgements bearing on the conduct of life. (Delaney C.F. 2001)

Poetry can contain wisdom in this general sense of sound judgements bearing on the conduct of life. Rhyming proverbs, or aphorisms, or longer poems can encourage thoughtful responses in readers. The readers rather than the author must be the judge of the depth of wisdom in a poem.

The author wrote a four-line aphorism summing-up his thinking about his foundational values in action-research for an e-discussion on values in research:

> Of course, justice is agape distributed.
> Chesed is the motivation for justice.
> Shalom is the fruit of justice.
> 'Image of God' is the ground of justice.

During an e-seminar on the Teacher-Researcher JISCMAIL[5] discussion site about publishing, the author tried to capture his thinking about preparing papers for publishing:

Audience is Everything
It might be a chore,
But who is this book for?
Lack of clarity here
Will, I fear
Lead to editor rejection
And writer dejection.

Another example of capturing thinking in a pithy verse is 'Loving-kindness'. It was written in a private e-mail

[5] https://www.jiscmail.ac.uk/cgi-bin/webadmin?A0=TEACHER-RESEARCHER (accessed 2 Jan 2012)

suggesting that the ancient wisdom of 'chesed' can be a foundational value of action research:

Loving-kindness

In a world of competition
'My rights' and self-assertion,
There's much to be said
For the Hebrew "chesed":
Loving-kindness,
Mercy and goodness,
Faithfulness, solidarity,
Steadfast love
Covenantally.

The energy flow…
Can you feel
The ancient wisdom
That we can know?

An aphorism is a 'pithy observation that contains a general truth' (OED). These verses were offered in the hope that readers may find the ideas of some value. A writer needs to be realistic about their own work. There is no room for hubris, making claims to deep wisdom. The compact, compressed expression and form of the verse might contain thought-provoking ideas for some readers as they reflect on the words. On some occasions, I receive little feed-back to these poems, but on others I receive warm comments about help received or for the ideas expressed. Occasionally I have had sharp retorts from offended or challenged readers.

The next poem was written by the author addressing himself, which arose out of painful experiences of tension in a relationship. Poetic reflection can distil wisdom for the writer of the poem:

Everyone should be ... slow to speak

In my words said:
'Shalom', 'Chesed'
To peace and loving-kindness
Add righteousness.

Careful consideration,
No provocation:
'As we wish to be treated',
Agape's not conceited.

In words clearly uttered,
(Or merely muttered),
Not in anger, being rude,
When hurting or in a mood.

Bridging and building,
Not breaking or wounding,
But loving appreciation,
And reconciliation.

At this point, there might well be questions buzzing around our minds like 'On what basis are words considered to be wise?' What are the criteria for 'sound judgement'? Can we only talk of choosing wisely, rather than of wise choices in post-modern secular society? Who decides whether we conduct our lives wisely? How is this wisdom constituted, and what is its nature and justification?

One might say that wisdom or wise choices lie in a technical sense of effective 'means to an end'. On this view, wisdom might be acting in a way that brings about desired or preferable goals or outcomes.[6] The problem here is that the desired ends may be disputable, of dubious worth, or self-interest. Also, the means of

---

[6] http://plato.stanford.edu/entries/pragmatism/ (accessed 3 January 2012). This website gives a full exposition of Pragmatism, and an in depth discussion of its nature, historical development and leading philosophers.

bringing about an effective or good end might be questionable. The criteria for wisdom on this view would be the consequences of action[7], rather than motive, or intrinsic good.

Might wisdom lie in actions that bring about the greatest good for the greatest number? [8] There is much merit in organising schools or institutions like The National Health along these lines for the common good. One problem might be that individual needs can be overlooked. Another is that a 'higher good' can be eclipsed by the greatest good for the greatest number. For example, the idea of service to the public might not be an acceptable organisational principle to all the directors for the culture of a bank. Reciprocity, or shareholders' or wider stakeholder interests might be wiser as the greatest good for the greatest number. A school imposing a rigid policy of equal opportunities for all may rule out providing for the needs of the most able or learners with special needs. The inclusion agenda, and priority of human rights in some organisations in UK recently has ruled out individual freedom to practice the Christian faith by wearing a cross, or praying for clients. Some might say that wisdom lies in enlightened self-interest. Is wisdom only doing that which is right, beneficial or effective in our own eyes? Does wisdom lie in self-preservation and self-interest? What then of the interests of the wider community beyond myself, my family, and friends?

There is a tradition of thinking in the Bible about the nature of wisdom. The Wisdom tradition comes with a

---

[7] http://en.wikipedia.org/wiki/Consequentialism (accessed 3 January 2012). "the consequences of one's conduct are the ultimate basis for any judgment about the rightness of that conduct. Thus, from a consequentialist standpoint, a morally right act (or omission) is one that will produce a good outcome, or consequence".

[8] See wide range of resources at http://utilitarianism.com/ (accessed 3 January 2012)

set of assumptions. There is a world-view underlying, supporting and justifying its understanding of 'wisdom', wise decisions, and 'sound judgements bearing on the conduct of life'.

The Book of Proverbs opens with these words:

> The proverbs of Solomon, son of David, king of Israel:
> To know wisdom and instruction,
>> to understand words of insight,
> to receive instruction in wise dealing,
>> in righteousness, justice, and equity;
> to give prudence to the simple,
>> knowledge and discretion to the youth-
> Let the wise hear and increase in learning,
>> the one who understands obtain guidance,
> to understand a proverb and a saying,
>> the words of the wise and their riddles.
> The fear of the Lord is the beginning of knowledge;
>> Fools despise wisdom and instruction.
>
> (Proverbs 1,1-7. English Standard Version)[9]

The 'fear of the Lord' is the lens through which the Wisdom literature should be read.[10] It is interesting that the writer of Proverbs in this introduction associates a range of words with wisdom: instruction, understand, insight, wise dealing in righteousness, justice and equity, prudence, knowledge, discretion, learning, guidance, instruction. Wisdom encompasses a wide range of concepts and activity, but it is informed by "The fear of the Lord". The source of wisdom lies in God.

---

[9] Scripture quotation from *The Holy Bible*, English Standard Version published by HarperCollins Publishers c. 2001 by Crossway Bibles, a division of Good News Publishers. Used by permission. All rights reserved. This version 2002. London.

[10] See Wisdom and Covenant by Grant J.A. in *Dictionary of the Old Testament. Wisdom Poetry & Writings*. Ed. Longman III T. & Enns P. 2008. Nottingham: IVP

Goetzmann J. discusses the original Hebrew and Greek words for 'wisdom'[11] illustrating that words for wisdom have been variously translated 'teach', 'instruct', 'to reason out', 'devise craftily', 'understanding', 'knowledge', 'chastening', 'disciplining', 'exhortation', 'insight', 'prudence', 'straight', 'right'. He says:

> 'One must note the spread of meaning in the word-group. Sophia denotes specialist knowledge in a particular field, such as handicraft, or in art…but equally in economic shrewdness (Proverbs 8,18,21), the art of government (Prov. 8,13), or education. Over and above this, it is concerned quite generally with the sagacious behaviour which enables a man to master life (Prov. 8,32-36). Here it depends on right conduct in obedience to the will of God rather than on theoretical insight. Wisdom is accordingly connected with the fear of Yahweh: "The fear of the Lord is the beginning of wisdom and the knowledge of the Holy One is insight" (Prov. 9,10; Job 28,28). Here also is developed the distinctive aspect of understanding of wisdom in Israel: wisdom is rooted in adherence to God".

He notes that there are astonishing parallels between Proverbs 22,17-23,11 and the Egyptian Wisdom of Amenemope. He comments that in adopting these texts Israel brought them firmly into line with its own religious convictions.

As Estes explains[12], in the Wisdom books for the most part, 'God communicates through general revelation. Humans are challenged to observe Yahweh's world and reflect upon his imbedded moral order in his creation so that they can derive lessons for life' (Prov.

---

[11] *The New International Dictionary of New Testament Theology Volume 3.* 'Wisdom' p. 1026-1033

[12] Estes D.J. 2008. 'Wisdom and Biblical Theology' in *Dictionary of Old Testament. Wisdom, Poetry & Writings.* Ed by Longman 111 T., & Enns P. 2008. Nottingham: IVP

6,6-11; 24,30-34). Wisdom, knowledge and skill come ultimately from God: the smith's skills at his forge (Isaiah 54,16), or the farmer. 'God instructs him and teaches him the right way... all this comes from the Lord Almighty wonderful in counsel and magnificent in wisdom' (Isaiah 28,26-29). Estes develops this world-view of the Wisdom literature further based on the fear of the Lord.[13]

As I was feeling my way towards an understanding of how poems can reflect the category of 'wisdom', and how this genre of Biblical writing can provide a background to interpreting some of this author's poems I came across Hubbard's articles on 'Wisdom' and 'Wisdom Literature' in *The New Bible Dictionary* (Hubbard D.A. 1962). I acknowledge the help and conciseness of these articles on which I have been drawing extensively.

He says that wisdom in the Old Testament is intensely practical. It is the art of being successful, and the forming of correct plans to achieve desired results. He quotes possessors of technical skill being called 'wise': Bezaleel chief artisan of the Tabernacle; professional mourners; navigators, and shipwrights as possessors of wisdom. Kings and leaders were in special need of wisdom: David and Solomon were granted 'wisdom' to deal with their official duties. Dr Hubbard goes on to explain how the messianic King predicted in Isaiah would be equipped with wisdom (Isaiah 9,6.). (quoting Porteous N.W.1955[14]). He goes on to explain how a special class of wise men and women arose in the Monarchy to formulate workable plans, and to prescribe advice for successful living. There is a helpful paragraph about wisdom in the fullest sense belonging to God. He says of Biblical wisdom:

---

[13] See p. 857 of above.
[14] See http://home.paonline.com/ahanna/HTML/Wisdom%202.htm (accessed 4 Jan 2012)

"Stemming from the fear of the Lord it branches out to touch all of life. Wisdom takes insights gleaned from the knowledge of God's ways, and applies them in the daily walk"

"…instructions for successful living are given or the perplexities of human existence are contemplated" p.1333-4.

The types of wisdom literature are explained: short, pithy, proverbial sayings for personal happiness and welfare; and wisdom monologues or dialogues which attempt, 'to delve into such problems as the meaning of existence, and the relationship between God and man. This speculative wisdom is practical and empirical, not theoretical'. Dr Hubbard mentions the Wisdom literary devices of poetic parallelism, comparisons, numerical sequences, alliteration, acrostic patterns, riddles, parables, and allegories.[15]

Of course, modern poetry is non-canonical, lacks the quality of being God-breathed, and is not clothed with the same authority. Nevertheless, it can reflect the Wisdom category or genre, and seek to take insights from natural revelation, and the revealed Word of God, and then apply them to contemporary situations.

The next three poems illustrate the style of Wisdom literature where the reader is encouraged to pause, contemplate, perhaps smile, but certainly give thought to the subject matter. The reader can make connections, relating the wisdom of the text to current situations.[16] It may be a proverbial short pithy saying, a longer passage, or a discourse.

---

[15] P.1334-5. *The New Bible Dictionary* op.cit.

[16] Hebrew for proverb: 'masal' : likeness or similitude. See Hildebrandt T. 2008 'Proverb, Genre of' and Longman iii T. 2008 'Proverbs 1: Book of' in *Dictionary of The Old Testament. Wisdom, Poetry & Writings*. Nottingham: IVP. This author found the articles p.528-552 informative and illuminating.

The first poem is a cell-phone or 'mobile' telephone conversation, illustrating how ordinary telephone social interaction can deteriorate.

Gossip? Surely not?
(an imaginary conversation on the phone)

"Hello,
How are you?
Have you heard…?
Did you know…?"

"I'm glad
You are well".
"Life's just mad!".
"I rang to tell…"

"Did you see
What she was wearing…?
"…Yes, she's expecting"
"…And what about the preacher…
"A good looking teacher!"

"Gossip…?
What me?
I just like to see,
Know what's going on:
Friends with everyone."

The second entitled Envy has a similar intention, to cause readers to stop and think:

Envy
(mobile telephone conversations…)

"Hello again!
It's me.
Sorry to be a pain…"
But can we
Come to you?"
"…Your garden's
Bigger too."

"A larger barbecue…?"
"…You bought it new…?"
(It must be nice
To afford that price.
Ours we found and
Bought in Poundland!"

"So you'll soon be flying
To a flat you're hiring?"
"Algarve you say?"
(That'll be the day
I get one holiday
On my husband's pay!)

"You heard the pastor's talk
On envy and the Christian walk?"
"…I guess if it applies
We'll take notice if we're wise".
"But ENVY? That's not me!"
(Just a hint of jealousy!)

The third poem is called 'Stealing?' It is an imaginary conversation with one's own conscience as a meditation on the eighth Commandment:

Stealing?

Only borrowing
And forgetting
Not returning.
Not intentionally
Stealing, depriving
Owners wilfully.

Stealing?
A reputation
A false accusation,
Subtle suggestion
Just gossiping,
Not assassination
Character destroying.

Stealing?
   Everyone does it.
   Using Company I.T.
   For something private,
   Claiming expense
   Adding just a bit
   Round-up a few pence.

Stealing?
   A financial phase:
   Saving tax these days,
   In whatever ways
   Maximize profit
   No need to stop it?

These poems were written with the hope that they speak wisdom to readers who are willing to listen.

'Consumer Detox' was written as a response to an article on the LICC (London Institute for Contemporary Christianity) blog 'Connecting With Culture': 'What Shape are you in?' by Mark Powley.[17] It uses the literary devices of rhyming couplets, irony, and allusions to Biblical texts. The author hoped that readers would pause and think about the consumerism that grips us, about how we can be defined by what we buy, and how we are squeezed into a mould.

Consumer Detox

I am a consumer.
The more I buy, the sooner
We come out of recessions,
In praise of possessions.

The untransformed mind
Is clearly defined

---

[17] http://www.licc.org.uk/email/221
(accessed February 7th 2011)
Licc London Institute for Contemporary Christianity:
http://www.licc.org.uk/ (accessed 4th January 2012)

'I am, because I buy',
No need to ask 'Why?'

I may be squeezed
But don't want to be freed.
It's much too bold
To replace the mould.
The social norm
Is to closely conform.
It takes faith and grace
To give His image space.

'Empty Pool Syndrome' was written as a response to an e-discussion on 'leadership in Christian thinking'. It uses the literary devices of sustained metaphor and allusion to rich Christian images of 'Living Water', 'parched land', 'vineyards', 'cultivation', and 'fountain'. The first stanza which is unrhymed poses the key question, then subsequent stanzas use an 'ing' rhyming scheme to portray breathless activity. The final verse concludes with a question to prompt reflective thinking.

Empty Pool Syndrome

Has that Living Water
That well, springing up,
Refreshing parched land
Become an empty pool?

We've been taking care
Of other vineyards:
Planning and organising,
Clearing and digging,
Employing and supervising,
Sowing and pruning,
Fertilizing and weeding,
Spraying and harvesting.

But our own vineyards
We've been neglecting,
Our own advice unheeding.

Weeds have been growing,
Ditches blocking,
No longer irrigating,
The good fruit spoiling.

In all our hearing and listening,
Absorbing, reflecting, exploring,
Planning and articulating,
Envisioning and evaluating,
Explaining and clarifying,
Empathizing and discriminating,
Supporting and enabling:
The pool has run dry.

Do we need some gardening,
Radical renovating,
Restoring, refreshing,
Re-filling. reinvigorating:
By The Fountain of Life-giving?

The author wrote 'Seven Deadly Sins' as a parody[18] on the model of Proverbs 31,10-31: 'The Woman Who Fears The Lord'.[19] As a result of a correspondent expressing concern that the poem had chauvinistic dimensions, this author wrote 'Male Leadership'. Each stanza picks up one of a series of seven possible deadly sins of male leadership in Christian contexts, and wider society.

Male Leadership

(A meditation on Colossians chapter 3.)

From seven deadly sins or more:
Good Lord deliver us

From arrogance
And competitive pride

---

[18] 'an imitation of the style of a particular writer, artist, or genre with deliberate exaggeration for comic effect' Concise OED. Op cit.
[19] See this author's chapter 'Poetry and Humour'.

In our own ability,
We'll put on humility.

From grasping greed
And lust for power:
I'll practice gentleness
Tolerance and kindness.

I'll replace anger,
Malice, slander,
With forgiveness
Patience and righteousness.

Am I one who aspires
To control my desires
Rejecting temptation
Denying gratification?

It's true I exaggerate
Add spin at any rate,
The truth distorting,
Not overtly lying.

My orthodox Biblicism
Is Beyond any criticism.
My objectivity
Avoids sin of popularity.

I have an expectation
Of a large congregation,
Delegating love and care
To those more pastorally aware.

This poem takes the key ideas of the text in Colossians and applies them to a contemporary scene of possible temptations of male leadership in Christian organisations and perhaps to leadership roles more widely.

The next poem 'Flames of The Brokenness of Britain' starts with a portrayal or poetic narrative about the urban riots that shocked the British nation in Summer 2011. The second verse reflects the comments made by interpreters in the press, and points to the need for refilling society's moral reservoirs. The poem concludes invoking the Ten Commandments and example and teaching of Christ as a way to peace and harmony. The appeal of the poem for returning to Christian values reflects the wisdom of King David in Psalm 19, 7-11:

> The law of the Lord is perfect,
>> Reviving the soul:
> The testimony of the Lord is sure
>> Making wise the simple…
> Moreover, by them is your servant warned;
>> In keeping them there is great reward' [20]

Flames of The Brokenness Britain

Protesting
Became rioting
Larceny and looting
Brazen burglary
Flames of fury
Leaping to safety
Burning business
Fear and distress.
'Free pickings!'
'Choose your store'
'Come for more,
You urban poor'!
Bring alienation
Criminal agitation.
Opportunities serve
Grab what you deserve!

Cameron's 'Brokenness of Britain'
Is debated by the politician:
Causes and blame;

[20] English Standard version of the Bible, 2002, London: HarperCollins.

Issues to name.
Why in all classes such greed
'Bankers', MP's acquisitive need?
'We must have it';
'Because you're worth it'
Symbols of success.
'What I have' materialism
Insatiable consumerism.
Is there a moral collapse?
'Reservoirs' running dry perhaps,
Refreshing water has been polluted
Values questioned and disputed?
With all our secular analysis
Social and community crisis,
Do we need to 'unblock those streams'
Revive our spiritual and moral dreams?

'The Moral Code once advertised
Forgotten or just despised
Showed people honesty, truthfulness,
Love of neighbour, and faithfulness,
Community and fellowship,
Ground for our citizenship.
Christ implanted in our mind
Ideas of a sacrificial kind.
This reservoir needs refilling
Not abandoning or rejecting.
The way to peace and harmony
Flourishing and opportunity
Is not by social tinkering
But God's justice in our thinking.

'Storms of Doubt' was written in May 2011 after the massive tornadoes struck communities in the USA. It echoes one of the themes of suffering in the book of

Job (on which Walton comments:[21] 'It's literary quality and compelling characters have made it one of the most sublime master pieces of ancient literature'). The poem echoes the Wisdom motif of theodicy, vindication of divine providence in view of the existence of puzzling evil or undeserved suffering.

Storms of Doubt and Faith

The dark funnel cloud
Swirling, roaring loud,
Destroying, crushing, sweeping
All in its chaotic path.
A dreadful demon of wrath
Leaving devastation,
And a child's question:
'Why did God make
These tornadoes?'

How can we answer
The issues we pose?
Does this bring about
A whirlwind of doubt?
Beyond man's opinion
God remains sovereign,
Beyond my comprehension.
So, what is faith's deduction:
Providence,[22] not harsh retribution,
A flawed and fallen Creation
Waiting for transformation
In the Reconstruction
Longing for justice, redemption
On the Day of Resurrection.

[21] Job 1: The Book of. Walton J.H. 2008 in *Dictionary of the Old Testament, Wisdom, Poetry & Writings*. Eds Longman III T. & Enns P. 2008. Nottingham: IVP.
[22] See Grudem W. 1994 p.315-354 *God's Providence* (in Systematic Theology). Leicester: IVP

One characteristic of the book Ecclesiastes (with its words like 'goads' and 'nails') is the thought-provoking 'questions' posed by the writer, appealing to the mind of the listener or reader, followed by comments:

"What gain has the worker from his toil?" 3,9.
"Who knows whether the spirit of a man goes upwards and the spirit of the beast goes down into the earth? 3,21
"For what advantage has the wise man over the fool?" 6,8.

Comments or observations follow the questions posed.

I have followed this pattern in 'How Can We Remain Silent?' written as a response to Fraser Nelson's article in the British *Daily Telegraph* on December 23rd 2011, 'How can we remain silent while Christians are being persecuted?' Questions are raised, readers invited to respond, then statements or points are made in the second stanza about the contrast between freedoms and tolerance in the UK and the restrictions and persecutions in some Islamic societies like Iran and Pakistan.[23] The final verse makes an appeal for lovers of freedom to speak-out.

How Can We Remain Silent?

Is neutrality and silence
Appropriate when such violence
Is perpetrated by some regimes,
Persecution by various means:
Threats, ill-treatment, bombings,
Arrests, forfeiture of belongings
Against the followers of The Way
By Muslims that are led astray?

The tolerance of an open-society
Is unknown to the Islamic majority

---

[23] See for current information and news
http://barnabasfund.org/

On the 20-30 latitude line
And east of Israel/Palestine.
Yet Muslims practice faith here
Without suppression or state fear.

We need to speak out freely
Against injustice in society,
And plead for the liberty
Of Christians in captivity.

In this chapter, I have attempted to make a case for the possibility of viewing poems echoing or reflecting the biblical tradition of Wisdom writings. Some illustrations of my writing were of short terse lines. Other poems are imaginary conversations or dialogues. I have also illustrated the genre of raising questions followed by a commentary. Proverbs in the English sense have not been included (e.g. 'Too many cooks spoil the broth', or 'Make hay while the sun shines'), but I have drawn on the wider range of writing genres in the Book of Proverbs. Of course, the reader will be the judge of whether these poems have elements of wisdom and whether the ideas contained can be related to contemporary life with any benefit.

In conclusion, I want to comment on Wisdom in the New Testament. The motifs of Wisdom writings that Klingbeil G.A. (2008) notes[24] continue in the New Testament: 'God is in control'; 'A godly life is a happy life'; 'The building of God's house'; and 'Paradise regained'. James Strong[25] lists fifty three references to 'wisdom' in the New Testament, and fifty six references to 'wise'. The Book of James is full of practical wisdom about matters of faith and behaviour. The writer speaks powerfully about Wisdom:

---

[24] Wisdom and History. *Article in Dictionary of Old Testament. Wisdom,Poetry and Writings*. Op.cit.

[25] *Strong's Exhaustive Concordance* Strong J. 1983. Grand Rapids, Michigan: Baker Book House

'Who is wise and understanding among you? By his good conduct let him show his works in the meekness of wisdom… But the wisdom from above is first pure, then peaceable , gentle, open to reason, full of mercy and good fruits, impartial and sincere. And a harvest of righteousness is sown in those who make peace'. James 3, 13-18 ESV.

There appear to be links between Jesus and Old Testament Wisdom in his preaching, and controversies with the Scribes. Paul teaches that Christ is the wisdom of God in contrast to the false reasoning of the contemporary Roman world:

'For the word of the cross is folly to those who are perishing, but to us who are being saved it is the power of God' 1 Corinthians 1,18-19. ESV.

Paul develops the theme of Wisdom in the ensuing verses.

'He is the source of your life in Christ Jesus, whom God made our wisdom and sanctification and redemption' 1, 30.

In the letter to the Colossians Paul enlarges on the wisdom theme:

'…to reach all the riches of full assurance of understanding and knowledge of God's mystery, which is Christ, in whom are hidden all the treasures of wisdom and knowledge' Colossians 2, 2-3 ESV.

The New Testament writers view Jesus as the epitome of wisdom, wiser than Solomon (Luke 11,31). In a dispute with opponents Jesus is associated with the personification of wisdom of Proverbs: "Wisdom is proved right by her actions", (Matthew 11, 18-19). In Proverbs 8 Wisdom is the firstborn of creation, and in Colossians 1,15-17 "Jesus is the image of the invisible God the firstborn over all creation. For by him all things were created…" The prologue to John's Gospel resonates with ideas from Proverbs 8. In Revelation 3,14 Jesus is the faithful and true witness the beginning of God's creation. There is a subtle allusion that Jesus now stands in the place of the personification "I, wisdom" of Proverbs 8.

There is insufficient space here to enlarge on this, but Jesus is Lord of all created reality, as well as the Church. So, in writing about matters of faith and any aspect of created reality, or area of human experience, as a Christian poet, this author needs to acknowledge Jesus as Lord, the Wisdom of God. I stand in the shadow of the tradition of Wisdom relating the key ideas of the Bible narrative of Creation-Fall-Redemption-Consummation to contemporary life.

The final two poems speak of wisdom available through general and special revelation. Christians can be informed by wisdom gained through natural revelation by studying all of reality, or particular forms or modes of Creation. The poet can draw on this wisdom and communicate through poetic structures and phrasing.

Forms of Knowledge

By systematic reflection
On the 'modes' in Creation,
Truth can be uncovered,
Wisdom can be discovered.

We can also explore the special revelation of the Bible, and proclaim the wisdom we discover there.

Revealed Religion

Not by ancient sophistry
Or modern philosophy,
Nor by meditation,
Rather by revelation;
Not by human endeavour
But God's own self-disclosure.

I conclude with words of the writer of Proverbs:

"Let the wise add to their learning"
Proverbs 1,5.

"Out in the open wisdom calls aloud,
She raises her voice in the public square"
Proverbs 1,20.[26]

---

[26] New International Version. 2011. London: Biblica and Hodder & Stoughton

References

English Standard version of the Bible 2002 London: HarperCollins.

Estes D.J. 2008. 'Wisdom and Biblical Theology' in *Dictionary of Old Testament. Wisdom, Poetry & Writings.* Ed by Longman 111 T., & Enns P. 2008. Nottingham: IVP

Goetzmann J. 1978 'Wisdom' in *The New International Dictionary of New Testament Theology Volume 3.* Ed. By Brown C. Exeter: The Paternoster Press.

Grant J.A. 2008 'Wisdom and Covenant' in *Dictionary of the Old Testament. Wisdom Poetry & Writings.* Ed. Longman III T. & Enns P. 2008. Nottingham: IVP

Hildebrandt T. 2008 'Proverb, Genre of' in *Dictionary of the Old Testament.* Ed. Longman III & Enns P. 2008. Nottingham: IVP.

Holy Bible. New International Version. 2011 London: Biblica and Hodder & Stoughton

Hubbard D.H. 1962 'Wisdom' and 'Wisdom Literature' in Douglas J.D. 1965 Ed. *The New Bible Dictionary.* Nottingham: IVP.

Klingbeil G.A. 2008 'Wisdom and History' in *Dictionary of The Old Testament, Wisdom, Poetry & Writings* Ed. Longman III T. & Enns P. 2008. Nottingham: IVP.

Longman III T. 2008 'Proverbs 1: Book of' in *Dictionary of The Old Testament. Wisdom, Poetry & Writings.* Nottingham: IVP.

Porteous N.W. 1955 'Royal Wisdom' in *Wisdom in Israel and in the Ancient Near East*, ed. M. Noth and D. Winton Thomas, E. J. Brill, Leiden 1955

Strong J. 1983. *Exhaustive Concordance*. Grand Rapids, Michigan: Baker Book House.

Walton J.H. 2008 'Job 1: The Book of' in *Dictionary of the Old Testament, Wisdom, Poetry & Writings*. Eds Longman III T. & Enns P. 2008. Nottingham: IVP.

Questions for Reflection:

Greenwich Observatory. Photo: the author

1. What do the words 'wise' or 'wisdom' mean?

2. Why are some of the books of the Bible called 'Wisdom Literature'?

3. In what way can a poem contain wisdom?

4. Look back through the poems and identify an example of wisdom in a poem.

5. What difference does the 'Fear of the Lord' make to wise sayings or wisdom in poetry?

6. Select a line or section from one of the author's poems then explain how it is helpful or contains some wisdom.

7. What place does wisdom have in your culture?

CHAPTER 6

The ANATOMY of POETRY

Author's photo of roses at Mottisfont Abbey.
Early summer.

The ANATOMY of POETRY

In this chapter I want to explore the anatomy, the form, and the structure of some of my poems, and the process involved in writing. I describe how sometimes when writing, ideas, thoughts and recollections 'tumble-out' of my mind into their own form. Some poems are a series of pictures that freeze a scene or recall experiences. The lyrical language captures the emotions of the moment. Others were written by squeezing ideas into a pre-determined structure. Some are constrained by an experimental form like a cross. It is strange how some are written in the inspiration of a few minutes, but others needed extensive research on content. They involve disciplined hard work on structure over a period of days or even weeks.

So what can be said generally about the nature of poetry? The Poetry.org website has a helpful comment on 'What is Poetry?'[1]

'poetry may use condensed or compressed form to convey emotion or ideas to the reader's or listener's mind or ear; it may also use devices such as assonance and repetition to achieve musical or incantatory effects. Poems frequently rely for their effect on imagery, word association, and the musical qualities of the language used. The interactive layering of all these effects to generate meaning is what marks poetry'... 'Perhaps the most vital element of sound in poetry is rhythm. Often the rhythm of each line is arranged in a particular meter.

[1] http://www.poetry.org/whatis.htm
(accessed 20th Nov. 2011)

Different types of meter played key roles in Classical, Early European, Eastern and Modern poetry. In the case of free verse, the rhythm of lines is often organized into looser units of cadence… Poetry in English and other modern European languages often uses rhyme. Rhyme at the end of lines is the basis of a number of common poetic forms, such as ballads, sonnets and rhyming couplets. However, the use of rhyme is not universal. Much modern poetry, for example, avoids traditional rhyme schemes'

The Wikipedia entry on poetry also says that it uses forms and devices such as assonance, alliteration, onomatopoeia, and rhythm that are sometimes used to achieve musical or incantatory effects.

'The use of ambiguity, symbolism, irony, and other stylistic elements of poetic diction often leaves a poem open to multiple interpretations. Similarly, metaphor, simile, and metonymy create a resonance between otherwise disparate images – a layering of meanings, forming connections previously not perceived'[2]

When I am reading or writing poetry it is usually the ideas in a poem that dominate my thinking rather than the form, shape, and technical aspects of poetics. While I can be impatient with some poems, passing over them quickly, others command attention. Some grip my imagination, or present a challenge. Reading a poem can make a claim on me, as I enter a new sphere or look at the common place from a different viewpoint.[3] It is usually the content, a vivid image or description, or my entering into the ideas of the poem imaginatively that has the main impact. It is as if the structure is secondary,

[2] http://en.wikipedia.org/wiki/Poetry
(accessed 20th Nov. 2011)
[3] See p.49 Georgia Warnke discussing Gadamer's structure of 'game-playing'. *Hermeneutics, Tradition and Reason.* 1987

the medium of the message. However, of course content and form are inextricably linked and equally important.

Georgia Warnke explains Hans-Georg Gadamer's view that there is pedagogical element to art:

> 'It presents its objects in such a way that the understanding of its audience can be enhanced and it may be moved to change its life. Indeed in Gadamer's view… the experience of art is one in which the audience is necessarily taken up into the work, experiences it as authoritative and learns to view its own world in the light of the work of art. Aesthetic experience is thus itself a form of knowledge'[4] (Warnke G. 1987)

I hope some of my poems may have this affect on individual readers. Some poems are descriptive and expressive, some exploratory or reactive, but others have a pedagogical purpose. I am wishing to communicate ideas or new ways of looking, as in 'Am I Listening?' The author's intention was to get readers to stop and think about whether they really listen, or just hear. One e-mail I received said, "I'm not showing this to my wife. She's been saying this about me for years'!

Am I Listening…?

Have I just heard
A phrase or odd word?
Am I really listening
To what she is saying?
Or does it appear
I've only half an ear
Before rushing on
To what I'd begun,
Because I am creating
My reply while I'm waiting?

---

[4] See p.60 op cit Warnke G. 1987

Am I really 'hearing',
Open to receiving
The message behind
(I can uncover or find)
The words she's expressing?

Am I really receptive,
Can I see her perspective,
Or, in this do I fail
As a strong alpha male?
Do I check my understanding
Before solving and planning?
Do I show sympathy,
Or display enough empathy?
Does she go away feeling
It's no use her speaking?

Lord,
Teach me to hear,
And make it quite clear
I am genuinely listening,
Open, responsive, receiving,
Checking my interpretation
Of this conversation.

We may ask, 'What of the process and anatomy of the poem, its form and structure?'

I remember walking through a park, then up on to the Downs in Dunstable, UK thinking about 'listening'. I was reflecting about how often I am not really listening in a conversation, but busily making up my mind about what I want to say next at a convenient pause, or even impatiently talking 'across' another person. This can be particularly true in the somewhat authoritarian roles of the schoolteacher, or minister of religion who want to determine the 'ends', or process of learning. There may be the temptation to be less willing to listen attentively because of the importance of what they have to say. There may be a reluctance to allow other minds to collaborate in or determine the content and process of conversation or learning.

Ideas, phrases and words emerge in my mind, from experiences, and from my reading, which I jot down. The form and structure to this poem partly emerged by themselves, bubbling-up from my experiences of feeling 'un-heard'. I sat in the car on my return from the walk, and crafted the shape of the poem. I tried to phrase it obliquely rather than confrontationally, by speaking in the first person, writing to myself. I was reflecting about how far I am willing to listen? Do I put into practice the appropriate skills?

Some of the emotional power and motivation of the poem came from a frustrating experience, where I had to struggle assertively to express my point of view and felt that I was not being 'heard'. I felt some hurt, but also some guilt about my reaction. The poem acts as a catharsis for these feelings. I turned my reactions and feelings into a self-evaluation of relationships with other people. The insight that came to me privately, is shared publicly in the hope that the poem might 'speak' to others who are willing to 'hear' about their listening.

The conclusion was written as a prayer, which may assist some readers' receptivity. I have attempted to express the 'rushing on' through the metre in the first stanza. The second is more meditative with pauses indicated by question marks. The last two lines carry the 'punch'.

> 'Does she go away feeling
> It's no use her speaking?'

The last stanza, the prayer form, reflects some of the counselling competences of active listening and checking interpretation.

Hans Bertens in his helpful historical sweep of literary theory[5] writes:

'For many readers educated in the Anglo-American tradition, form and structure are not only things that are alien to their interests – they do not read literature to learn about form and structure – but actually threaten the experience of reading... they seem to undermine the spirituality and freedom of the novel or the poem that they are reading.'

He goes on to argue that Art cannot do without form, and that for example a poem, is an end product of decisions involving form and structure.

In the poem 'Mourning For Faith', I wrote in free verse about the funeral of my neighbour who died suddenly, not yet thirty. In the entry 'free verse' in the Princeton Encyclopaedia of Poetry[6] the writer explains:

'free verse claims and thematizes a proximity to lived experience. It does this by trying to replicate, project, or represent perceptual, cognitive, emotional, and imaginative processes. Lived experience and replicated process are unreachable goals, but nevertheless this ethos is what continues to draw writers and readers to free verse'[7]

The lived experience was the funeral at an ancient priory of a young man who died suddenly, unexpectedly. I came home with the images of the service fresh in my mind and captured these impressions in free verse. I have tried to reflect the mood, the shock and sadness, and portrayed an image of a generation adrift from their ancient cultural mooring of the Christian beliefs and values of the medieval priory. The reader can perceive

[5] Bertens H.2008 *Literary Theory*. Abingdon. UK: Routledge
[6] Preminger A. and Brogan T.V.E. 1993
[7] Quoted in *Poetry: The Basics* by Jeffrey Wainwright. 2004

my social commentary, my interpretation of a post-modern generation without a 'big' story.

Mourning For Faith

The ancient Priory
Was filled with mourners
Respectfully dressed in black,
Shocked by sudden death:
A young man snatched away.
Friends, work mates, family,
Were fairly youthful:
Blond hair, fresh-faced.
The 'Y' generation
Stumbling over prayers
Were ill-at-ease with hymns.
Faith, was a fading echo
In parents' popular music:
'Amazing Grace' with bag-pipes,
'Abide With Me',
'You'll Never Walk Alone'
Ring-out from the terraces.
But they had no 'Big Story'
Other than their memories,
Or 'Hello' magazine and 'Facebook'.

In the next poem 'Redeeming Criticism', I was responding to a re-reading of Hans Bertens's book.[8] The title of my verse is a word play. It is like an echo articulating on the one hand a critical reading of the chapters, but listening to myself for the response echo about how to 'redeem literary criticism'. I was relating faith to literary criticism, interpreting criticism in the light of theological insights. I was reflecting about 'critiquing the criticism' from the perspective of the 'big narrative', or 'God's Story' of Christianity: Creation-Fall-Redemption-Consummation in Reformed theology.

---

[8] Op.cit. 2008

The poem is dense, with the complex ideas of the book compressed and condensed into short lines. The 'tion' rhyme structure reflects the abstract nouns, the technical jargon of literary criticism that is difficult for the non-technical reader. For this author it is a concise summary in couplets of Hans Bertens' scholarly but helpful book, but to other readers it may seem esoteric or inaccessible.

Redeeming Criticism

Literary Criticism's clear attention
Moved away from 'the author's intention'
To a 'storehouse' cultural collection
Of the best of writers' expression
On our human nature and condition.
Formal structure was a pre-occupation,
Not interpretation and exposition,
But the grammar and semantic dimension,
Devices: language organization,
Then later to 'signs' and convention,
Structures, carriers of meaning in narration.

Is just focus on form a frustration
To the reader's imagination?
A poem's historical situation
Enriches our interpretation,
Reading with political appreciation
Of class, gender, and race iteration.
What of Post-structural revolution,
Post-modernism's deconstruction?
Is language unstable communication,
Our reading flawed by our perception,
Thwarting any interpretation?
Does 'power' need interrogation,
Ideology under suspicion,
Writers under a dispensation
A cultural contamination?
With focus on colonization,
Or on sexual marginalization,

Ecology and man's domination,
There's an attack on common assumption.
Is there space for Mandates of Creation
For the sacred in poetic redemption?

Now by way of contrast, I have included a poem written for an adult art group. As I explained in Chapter 1, I follow the seasons for inspiration for painting and often write a verse on the theme. The next poem 'Making Light of Winter' was written quite quickly one morning in preparation for the group. The sonnet form of fourteen lines provided a ready structure, and a discipline for writing. I can see now on re-reading, it starts with the personification of Autumn, then uses a metaphor of 'winter blows in'. Then there are colourful images of winter. In the last six lines, I introduce some ideas and symbols of faith: 'Light to darkness', the 'incarnation', and the metaphor of 'love melting our icy hardness'. We can be un-responsive to the amazing story of Christmas. The familiarity of the narratives can mask the wonder of truth of Charles Wesley's carol that we sing:

'Veiled in flesh the god-head see.
Hail the incarnate deity!
Pleased as man with men to well
Jesus our Immanuel'"[9]

There are layers of meaning in my poem. The title itself is a play on words. 'Making light' can connote 'down-playing' the unpleasant aspects, or, making illumination, finding truth or meaning in the issues and problems we face. The darkness can be a symbol of evil, and of suffering. Darkness can be the lack of the Light of the World, the illumination of truth that the Christian faith brings. It can be the bleakness of secular evolutionary atheism. Darkness also hints at the fear of cancer

---

[9]   http://en.wikipedia.org/wiki/Hark!_The_Herald_Angels_ Sing   (accessed 31 Dec 2011)

reoccurring for the author. The 'expectation overcoming fear', hints at looking forward to coming through surgery successfully, and of the Christian expectation that death is not the end but the beginning of bliss and the hope of the Restoration, the New Heavens and new (restored) Earth.

One reader wrote saying the poem had a different significance for her, describing the issues about trauma and faith in her family. So, a poem can be interpreted differently, and its meaning can be subjective, or apposite for a particular person's experience.

In a sense, interpretation is a matter for the reader, but perhaps not solely so as postmodernist critics claim. I have illustrated the intentions and historical relatedness of the author in my poem. But of course the meaning or interpretation of text is not confined to the author's intention.

Gadamer in discussing aesthetics and hermeneutics says that the reality of a work of art and its expressive power cannot be restricted to its original horizon. "The work of art is the expression of a truth that cannot be reduced to what its creator actually thought in it"[10]

Making 'Light' of Winter

After Autumn takes its feast
Of russets, and copper
Leaves fall, Winter proper
Blows in from North and East.
Hoar frost sparkling bright
Dresses conifers and sedge,
Hips and haws festoon the hedge,
And snow settles silently white.
Advent brings the Light to darkness,
Count-down Christmas preparation,
To celebrate the Incarnation,
When love melts our icy hardness.

---

[10] P.95-6 *Philosophical Hermeneutics*

So we welcome this New Year
Expectation overcoming fear.

In the next poem the sonnet form was a convenient way of making a personal response to Bishop Nazir-Ali's speech at the annual conference of the Christian Broadcast Council reported by Barnabus Fund.[11]

The Big Society

So, are we no longer a 'free' society
Where conscience is still respected?
The 'Christian Story' has been neglected.
'Secular Materialism', says Bishop Nasir-Ali
Seeks its own ideology to enforce:
Equality agenda, rights of a minority
Are imposed on the vast majority;
Tyranny of 'public' over 'private' discourse;
Abandoning of a normative view
Of marriage and life's sacredness;
Attacks on the 'unborn child' too.
Without restoration and work to address
The vacuum left by our Christian Story
There may be no unifying 'Big Society'.

The sonnet form abbacddcefefgg is used to reflect about events in the UK in 2010–11, and to make social comment, informed by a Christian faith. Recent events have raised questions about our 'free society' (such as the prosecution of two hotel owners for refusing a shared bed to a homosexual couple, the arrest of street preachers, the forbidding of the wearing of Christian symbols at work, and a doctor disciplined for bringing faith into his practise).[12] I write, questioning whether our democratic freedom has been endangered by the

---

[11] http://www.barnabusfund.org/britain-is-no-longer-a-free-society-bishop-nazir-ali.html (accessed 18/04/2011)

[12] See http://www.christian.org.uk/resources/religious-liberty/ (accessed 8 June 2011)

human rights and sexual equality agenda of politicians and the European Court in the first decade of this new century in Britain. The last couplet suggests the vacuum in social ethics needs filling by the Christian Story to help create unifying values for David Cameron's 'Big Society'.

My wife and I visited Mottisfont Abbey (near Stockbridge, Hants, UK) in early summer, when the rose gardens are at their most impressive. I wanted to capture the experience, and say a 'thank you' to the Head Gardener in a poem with a freer form. It is all too easy to feel that our routine tasks, our secular work is somehow less spiritual than professional ministry or mission. In this next poem, I recognise that the gardener's work is prayer. The colour and perfume speak praise to the Divine Gardener.

The gardens spoke to me of the Jewish temple: the outer court, the Holy Place, and the Holy of Holies. At Mottisfont there is a succession of doors in walls, through which the visitor passes to the third garden. There is a fountain and pool that reminded me of the laver where Jewish worshipers cleansed themselves. The visitors pass pillar roses at the entrance called the Pilgrim rose.

So it was not so much the form of the poem and its structure that were important, but the imagery, the alliteration, and symbolism that the writer saw. The gardener sent a response to this poem:

"A beautiful poem, and one that I would have been proud to compose! Thank you so much for sending it to me! The 'Pilgrim' roses in the allee approach were a deliberate choice, as I recognize that many people make Mottisfont at rose time a place of annual pilgrimage. This was my way of greeting them and welcoming all to our beautiful garden. It takes a poet to both recognize and appreciate such symbolism."[13]

To The Head Gardener At Mottisfont

There were pillar roses
Emerging from the dust,
Pointing the Pilgrim,
Filling the air with
The perfume of praise.
Then a courtyard of colour,
A doorway to delights
Filled with His ways:
Clematis, Aquilegia
Outrageous hues and tints,
Long lavender lanes.
Then through a portal:
To the Holy of Holies,
Intoxicating roses,
An acceptable aroma
Ascends to The Gardener.

The process of writing is not always conscious, chosen or deliberate. This poem was not so much a technical or mechanical process, fitting ideas into a pre-determined structure. It is more like a series of slides or digital images, a series of mental pictures, organised around the idea of praise to the gardener. I walk around the gardens in my mind, like an action replay, re-calling, and trying to express in language the beauty of the walled gardens, the planting, the radiant colours, and the intoxicating perfume[14]. As I reflected, the symbolism of the garden emerged, taking on a spiritual dimension.

In the next poem, The Dreaded Disease, I use simple couplets in a meditation on Matthew's account

---

[13] In a private e-mail
[14] Visitors are requested to refrain from smoking in the walled gardens so that the perfumes of the flowers can be fully appreciated unadulterated.

of the healing of a man with leprosy. I have tried to enter into the experience of the man. The metre attempts to lead the reader from pathos in the first eight lines to the excitement and liberation of healing.

The Dreaded Disease

This pustular infection
Led to isolation, rejection.
That dreadful morning
The truth was dawning:
Just a lesion on the face
Would lead to my disgrace,
Driven from family and home,
Living rough and alone.

A rumour was spreading
About healing and cleansing…
Then a young Rabbi stopped by,
So without thinking why
I ran up to him to be seen.
"LORD, you can make me clean."
He reached out and touched me,
Disfigured, "Be clean, but see
That you tell no one."
Immediately, the sores were gone!
I'll no longer be rejected
But loved and accepted!

I wrote a poem in a 'terza rima' form (aba bcb cdc etc)[15] to say thank you to Luton and Dunstable Hospital for my treatment while recovering from a major operation. It was given to the nursing staff on the ward, who expressed their appreciation. I can now see the effects of the anaesthetic on my mind in the clumsier construction, irregularity of metre, and line length, but I reproduce the poem to illustrate a different form and rhyming scheme. Poems have a magical way of recalling

[15] http://www.poets.org/viewmedia.php/prmMID/5794

experience, of bringing mental photographs flooding back:

Thank You

For your Reception,
For my treatment.
As a reflection
I'll leave this comment:
"I'm so grateful".
Here's testament:
Being so helpful
Through long nights;
Attentive, careful
About acute care plights;
For empathizing;
For tomato soup delights
When food was unappetising;
For servant leaders;
E.I. surprising;   (E.I. 'Emotional Intelligence')
Hippocratic believers;
Skills of Urology;
Microsurgery designers;
Wisdom in Oncology;
For scans and x-rays;
Drugs of Cardiology;
Recovery phase;
Practitioner optimists;
For a budget that stays
Within plans of pessimists;
For needles of Phlebotomy;
Alchemy of anaesthetists;
For the hospital economy;
Bright-eyed physiotherapy,
And wonders of biochemistry.

The next poem Joseph's Story has an irregular metre and inconsistent rhyme scheme but was written to capture atmospheres: the attraction of love; the confusion about Mary's pregnancy; and the resolution of anxiety through Joseph's dream. His story is under-emphasized in Christian writing and tradition. I have tried to feel my way into his situation as a meditation over a Christmas festival celebrations.

Joseph's Story

It was her smile
That warm glow
In her eyes that drew,
That let me know
She loved me too.
Eyes averted shyly,
Her long glossy hair
Covered modestly.
I became aware
Of her beauty
Veiled as we walked
And of my duty
As we talked
Of betrothal.

The sound of her voice
As she confessed
Gave little choice:
A child expected,
How could this be?
A story of Gabriel,
Not disloyalty,
Of a Messiah as well?
All so confusing!
Unwilling to put her to shame
In my musing
To protect her name,
Resolved to divorce quietly
No impropriety.

But in darkest night,
Not as I feared,
In blinding light

An angel appeared:
"Do not fear to take
Mary as your wife".
I was so relieved.
It was God's Spirit
From whom she conceived
As spoken by the prophet.
I honoured engagement.
So before consummation
After her confinement
We went for registration.

I attended a poetry workshop led by Ian McEwen[16] as a prize for a Central Bedfordshire Libraries poetry competition on the theme of Games. One of Ian's activities was to get us writing about a walk. He gave us a few minutes to write then introduced some onomatopoeic words one every so often that we had to include in the poem. The idea was to produce sharp contrasts in the conversational poem. I chose a beach walk that I could picture and feel in imagination at Studland Bay in Dorset, UK.

Beach Walk

We walked over the sands
Seaweed in our toes
Holding hands and smiling.
The tide was coming in
With surf pounding the stacks.
Great black-backed gulls
Glided across the waves.
We watched the flotsam
Moving up the beach:
Plastic and sour fruit

---

[16] http://www.happenstancepress.com/index.php?option=com_content&view=article&id=418:the-stammering-man-ian-mcewen&catid=53:sphinx-16-2011&Itemid=74 (accessed 31 Dec 2011)

Left by lazy picnickers.
Castles and fortress walls
Resisted the tide momentarily
But were washed by the waves
Collapsing, the sand oozing
With water and yellow scum.
A large bald man
Smoking a cigar
Spat on a child's bucket.
Disgusted, we climbed the steps
Entering the haven Café.

The next poem does not just capture vivid images in words, nor does it use lyrical devices to arouse emotional responses. It is a different genre, a style or category of poetry. 'How Can We Remain Silent?' asks questions, uses the language of rational discourse. It is more polemic in nature, more political, seeking to influence and persuade the reader. The first stanza of eight lines with four rhyming couplets reflects the issues raised in an article in the *Daily Telegraph* by Fraser Nelson about the persecution of Christians (December 23rd 2011. 'How can we remain silent while Christians are being persecuted?'). Each of the forms of persecution mentioned have been reported on the Barnabus mailings and e-bulletins[17]. So, each example mentioned is short-hand for a case study. The opening lines raise a challenge to political correctness, to tolerance, and 'avoiding giving offence' masquerading as the moral high ground rather than truth, or freedom of speech.

The second stanza points to the irony of Muslims experiencing freedom of belief and worship in the UK, but those freedoms being absent in Islamic societies with Shariah law that radical Islamists wish to impose on the free world. The crescents of the flames of

---

[17] http://barnabasfund.org/UK/News/Latest-emergencies/ (accessed 29 December 2011)

persecution flare in Islamic countries in an arc from Indonesia, Pakistan, Afghanistan and Iran to the countries north of the Sahara. Christians have been driven out of Iraq in their hundreds, and even the Arab Spring has brought new fears to Coptic Christians in Egypt, and believers in Syria.

Other voices see the power dimensions of these situations: Christians with the symbol of the cross of the Crusades, and the 'decadent western' imperialist colonizing powers that subjugated Muslim peoples are now themselves being ejected from their home countries. No doubt the solidarity that tribalism demands also plays a part. It is pay-back-time protest at Western foreign policy towards Palestine and 'occupations' of Muslim lands.

The final stanza makes a strong plea for not only Christians to speak out against persecutions and false accusations of 'blasphemy', but also for governments to express their dismay, and for the press to report persecution of Christians (The Press had been remarkably shy in their comments).

How Can We Remain Silent?

Is neutrality or silence
Appropriate when such violence
Is perpetrated by some regimes
Persecution by various means:
Threats, ill-treatment, bombings,
Arrests, forfeiture of belongings
Against the followers of The Way
By Muslims who are led astray?

The tolerance of an open society
Is unknown to the Islamic majority
On the 40-15 latitudes spine,
Or, East of Israel and Palestine.
Yet Muslims practice faith here
Without suppression or State fear.

We need to speak-out freely
Against injustice in society,
And plead for the liberty
Of Christians in captivity.

'Walk in the Vallee de Joux' was written as a series of mental photographs of a family walk in Switzerland in The Jura mountain air on a cold October morning in dazzling light. I wrote when we returned to the holiday apartment:

Walk in the Vallee de Joux

The children wrapped-up warm
Against the north-easterly
The cold cutting our faces.
We walked in long shadows,
The bright light illuminating
The trees in yellows and gold,
And artists' alizarin:
Birch, maple, ash and beech.
The mist hovered eerily
Above the long lake
Revealing glimpses
Of scattered chalets
Shrouded on the far shore.
The woods clung to contours
With hidden cabins and
Luxury apartments
Lining the Lake-side.
The white limestone
Beach dazzled in the daylight
And waves washed on the shore.

In this final poem for this chapter 'The Hobby at College Lake', I wrote without worrying about form. It has an irregular rhyme scheme, but employs assonance, (resemblance of sound of consonants in nearby words),[18] alliteration,(same letter or sound at the beginning of adjacent words)[19], onomatopoeia, (formation of a word from a sound associated with what is named)[20]. These literary devices are used to capture the scene. The poem clothes itself with an almost spiritual quality reflecting the exhilaration and joy of the author watching from a hide. The poem also has an underlying metaphor for the freedom of the human spirit and of the soul departing at death to Paradise in the line, "Preparing for his African flight'.

The Hobby at College Lake

The scimitar silhouette
Wheeled in the sky
Sweeping across the lake,
Suddenly diving,
Steeply swooping,
In its talons to take
The quartering dragonfly
On its own prey set.
The sheer speed
Across the beds of reed;
Mastery of the air:
A view comparatively rare;
Moustachioed, splendid sight
Preparing for his African flight.

In this chapter, we have been looking at the more technical aspects of poetry. I have emphasized the importance of the content of poems, and then explained aspects of the process of writing. Then there are illustrations of some of the components of form, and structure. I have highlighted examples of literary devices in the poems. Sometimes there is a pre-determined, conscious technical plan. Writing can be disciplined

---

[18] Definitions from *Concise Oxford Dictionary*

[19] Ditto

[20] Definition from *Concise Oxford Dictionary*

exhausting work. On other occasions the language just flows. Some nights I wake up with words, lines, phrases or images on my mind and have to capture them with a pencil before they fade. The anatomy of the poem can become more significant when I analyse what I have written. Sometimes I start out with a deliberate form or scheme, but on other days I am more conscious of form when I come to craft or polish the shape in the revising process.

There can be a "paralysis of analysis". It is interesting that Margaret Attwood said:

> "I don't want to know how I write poetry, paying attention to how you do it, is like stopping in the middle of any other totally involving and pleasurable activity to observe yourself suspended in the fatal inner mirror: you may improve your so-called technique, but only at the expense of your so-called soul"[21]

I hope that in writing this chapter I may have succeeded in the former 'improve your so-called technique', and avoided the latter ('at the expense of your so-called soul').

---

[21] Poetic Process by Atwood M. 1971 in A *Field Guide to Contemporary Poetry and Poetics*. Ed. Friebert S., Walker D. and Young D. 1997. Oberlin: Oberlin College Press.

References

Attwood M. 1971 Poetic Process, in *A Field Guide to Contemporary Poetry and Poetics*. Ed. Friebert S., Walker D. and Young D. 1997. Oberlin: Oberlin College Press.

Bertens H. 2008 *Literary Theory*. Abingdon. UK: Routledge

Gadamer H.G. 1976 (in Ling D.E. 1976 Trans. & Ed.) Philosophical Hermeneutics. Berkeley and Los Angeles: U. of California Press

http://www.barnabusfund.org/britain-is-no-longer-a-free-society-bishop-nazir-ali.html (accessed 18/04/2011)

http://www.christian.org.uk/resources/religious-liberty/ (accessed 8 June 2011)

http://en.wikipedia.org/wiki/Hark!_The_Herald_Angels_Sing

http://www.poetry.org/whatis.htm (accessed 22 June 2011)

http://www.poets.org/viewmedia.php/prmMID/5794 (accessed 22 June 2011)

Oxford English Dictionary (Concise) 2002. Oxford: O.U.P.

Preminger A. & Brogan T.V.F. (eds) 1993. *The New Princeton Encyclopedia of Poetry and Poetics*. Princeton: Princeton Univ. Press

Wainwright J. 2004. *Poetry: The Basics*. Abingdon: Routledge.

Warnke G. 1987 *Gadamer. Hermeneutics, Tradition, and Reason* Oxford and Cambridge: Polity Press in association with Blackwell

Questions for Reflection:

---

1. In poetry is it the content, the words, the topic that is more important, or is it the form, poetics and literary techniques ?

2. Identify two different literary forms the author has used in this chapter.

3. Give an example of how the poet has used techniques to emphasize the meaning of a poem.

4. Choose one poem that has a religious theme, and one that makes social comment. What do you like about the content, and the form?

5. What are the structures and forms of poetry in your culture, in your mother tongue?

CHAPTER 7

POETRY as a WAY of KNOWING

St. Aldhelm's Chapel
Photo: The author

St. Albans Head
It was a long and lonely walk
Out to the Purbeck headland,
A well-worn, but rocky path,
Stunted trees sheltered
From the Atlantic storms.
The Chapel stood foursquare
Against the westerly winds,
A memory to St. Aldhelm
Twelfth Century bishop,
Scholar and Dorset poet.
This dark, dank place,
Perhaps a chantry chapel,
The shrill wind singing
Masses for souls lost at sea.
Girls dropped pins here
Charms in hope of husbands.
But as I stood in the gloom
A radiance of light shone
Peace and hope of faith
And the shadow of the Cross
Lingered on the hard stone altar.

POETRY as a WAY of KNOWING, and a PROCESS and PRODUCT of RESEARCH

This chapter discusses poetry as a means of creative expression, and a way of knowing. It argues that poetry is a means and product of research. The author's own biographical experience of poetry is described briefly for context. He outlines how poetry can 'capture' experience, distil and compress ideas. He goes on to argue that poetry can be creative not only in artistic expression, but also as a reflective process creating ideas, and clarifying beliefs. Then he discusses poetry as a particularly powerful form of communication. The chapter concludes arguing that poetry can be a way of knowing, and a process and product of research. Each of the points discussed is illustrated by the author's own verse.

While I am aware that writing can be self-indulgent, a mild form of vanity, there is a sense in which this author is doing action-research on his own writing, seeking to understand the nature of poetry and to develop and improve his art form. I want to argue that Poetry can be a way of knowing, a space for a new way of speaking about experiences. As Wainwright says:

> "Poetry is a free space for rhetoric and imagination. It might be tightly argumentative or loosely associative. It can combine so many aspects of experience, knowledge and ways of speaking… Poetry works with ideas, but also within the subjective mystery of our consciousness, with the qualia of the mind… Its kinds are sometimes playful,

and sometimes deal with the words that engage the most serious topics we know"

(Wainwright J. 2004)

Introduction: Context

I grew-up as a child with the rhythm of poetry, through nursery rhymes and memorising the verses of Christian songs and hymns[1]. We read the musical language of the Authorised Version of the Bible, particularly the Psalms. My mother learned, and recited Christian verse publicly which I admired, amazed at her memory skills and confidence. The language of poetry was part of home life. We had a lot of fun at Christmas as children writing limericks as a party parlour game. We lived on an estate where each road was named after a poet: Masefield Avenue; Binyon Crescent; Kipling Place, and so on.

At school, we were introduced to the English Literature canon. As a boy, I remember enjoying what I thought was the more masculine poetry of John Masefield, and reciting Browning at a speech competition. Later I took English Literature for GCE 'A' Level and began to study Shakespeare, the Elizabethan Lyrics, and Keats' romantic poetry. The rich imagery of Keats was a delight. We struggled with Chaucer, and wrestled with Gerard Manley Hopkins. Then in my teacher-training I read Divinity and English Literature, learning more about the canon: Yeats, Pope, Metaphysical poets, Donne, Herbert, Vaughan and others, but was baffled by T.S. Eliot's Four Quartets. The visual images and forms of poetic expression

---

[1] Sankey I.D.1958 Sacred Songs and Solos.
Golden Bells Hymn Book 1970. London. Scripture Union (although we used an earlier edition)
Elim Choruses. (Still available on Amazon)
http://www.amazon.co.uk/Elim-Choruses-No-2/dp/B002L06I26 (accessed 20 Nov. 2011)

impacted my mind. I wrote a short dissertation on 'Faith and Scepticism in Modern Poetry' in the late 1960s.

I composed short poems for my girlfriend and future wife, and occasionally wrote while our children were growing up, but did not write more regularly or seriously until I retired from school teaching and management. Since then, I have been writing for pleasure, capturing experiences of the seasons and the natural world. I have composed verses for the Art group I help coordinate to introduce the themes for painting.[2] Some of my poems reflect on contemporary issues, and on events like the death of friends. Some were written more light-heartedly on experiences of medical treatment, and others for my grandchildren. Then there are more serious reflections on research methods, and on Christian Faith themes: festivals, suffering, and faith in society.

Firstly, Poetry as 'Capturing Experience'

Over the years, I have developed interest in communicating ideas as a teacher and writer. More recently, I have read more about genres of writing,[3] dipped into hermeneutics and meaning in written and spoken English. The discipline and process of writing verse attracts and intrigues. The use of imagination, thought and language, the forms and structure of poetry writing all provide a method and means of reflection and expression.

I think it was Ezra Pound[4] who likened poetry to a machine that captures experience. It is an imperfect

---

[2] See chapter 'Art and Poetry'
[3] e.g. Bertens H..2008 *Literary Theory. The Basics*. London: Taylor and Francis
Carson D.A. 1996. *The Gagging of God*. Leicester: Apollos. (Chapters 2-3).
[4] http://www.poetryfoundation.org/bio/ezra-pound (accessed December 2nd, 2011).

image, too mechanistic, but I like the idea of 'capture'. Poems can freeze and portray the colour, emotion, or delight of an experience, and make it available to the writer later so that rich memories come flooding back, or other readers can enter into the experience.

In this next poem, I have attempted to capture the delight of visiting Studland Bay in Dorset, UK on many occasions:

Studland Bay

From Corfe a winding road
Takes you over the heights
With harbour vistas: fleeting sights,
Down through the trees to the village shop
Where cyclist families like to stop,
Through pines where non-members pay
To park in this continental bay.
A short walk through fine sand,
Or follow paths on N.T.[5] land
Along the beach to the shallow sea
Where sea horses are swimming free,
The water Prussian blue or viridian
A climate almost Mediterranean;
Tree fringed beaches, seaweed reaches and
Harry's Rocks frame children's sand.

In Swyre Head I have tried to capture and express our experience of walking up the footpath to the highest point on the Dorset coast, using vivid images and a breathless rhythm:

Swyre Head, Dorset

The air was fresh, bracing,
Westerly facing,
Low clouds racing.
We walked up pacing,
Gradually ascending

---

[5] National Trust

Then stopped, panting,
Paused a while resting,
Turning around gazing
Over Corfe to Poole sun lighting,
The harbour illuminating.
We continued rising,
Swyre Head climbing,
Wind buffeting,
The panorama amazing!
We looked across Kimmeridge, indenting
Cliffs and inlets contending,
Weymouth and Portland fading.
To the east St Alban's Head appearing
Sea cloud misting
Below Hanstout, Encombe nestling.[6]

Poetry with its language, imagery and metaphor can express and capture a thought or insight of the moment, or be the result of extended reflection to make it available to the writer or other readers:

A Cotswold Church

"I saw the rainbow colours, sparkle, falter
Refracted light across the altar.
Reality windowed, illuminated by the sun,
Each colour as an aspect of the whole, the One.
The prism of human understanding
Wishes to divide, control, reducing
One light into 'aspects', 'disciplines' or 'forms',
Each separate: content, concepts, methodology,
   norms.
The beauty of that ancient art
Spoke wisdom to my mind and heart."

---

[6] Some of these poems are available on
http://allpoetry.com/ (accessed 2nd December 2011), and
others were on http://christianpoetry.org/
(site now closed)

There is a sense in which poetry represents not just thought in a moment of time, but thoughts based on all of the experience, reading and thinking of a lifetime so far. Life experience and reflection is the data and interpretation on which writing is grounded.

Secondly, Poetry Compresses and Distills Ideas and Experience

In 'A Cotswold Church' I am compressing and distilling a long period of reflection about areas of human experience, forms of knowledge, modes of reality as the basis for designing a secondary school curriculum. I was wanting to compress and distil this and communicate it in a seminar with post-graduate teacher-trainees about forms of knowledge, areas of reality of the whole of God's Creation.

The writers have expressed it well when they say, poetry

'may use condensed or compressed form to convey emotion or ideas to the reader's or listener's mind or ear; it may also use devices such as assonance and repetition to achieve musical or incantatory effects. Poems frequently rely for their effect on imagery, word association, and the musical qualities of the language used. The interactive layering of all these effects to generate meaning is what marks poetry'[7]

"At its best, poetry is the distillation of language and experience into their rhythmic and thematic elements"[8]

Distilling is not just a process of purifying by heating and vaporising, cooling and condensing to make spirits.

[7] From 'What is poetry?' http://poetry.org/whatis.htm (accessed March 29th 2011).
[8] Jay Hovdey, http://www.drf.com/news/book-poetry-captures-essence-19th-century-hero-isaac-murphy (accessed March 29th, 2011)

Nor is it just 'extracting the essential meaning'. There is a sense in which the metaphorical 'heat', 'vaporising' of life experience, and the condensing of reflective thought and meditation can be used by the Spirit to purify, and to extract meaning.

In 'Spirit of the Swan' I have attempted to capture experiences of watching swans on Lake Geneva and Tring Reservoirs, distilling not just the drama of swans taking flight, but deeper layering of the pain and suffering in life, and the soul's struggles before rising to eternal life.

The illustration below is another example of cards I use to introduce painting topics to an adult art group:

Spirit of The Swan

What grace! What elegance!
Gliding with imperial stance;
Paddles nonchalant, brave
Against the incoming wave.
At some inner call or light
Instinctive exilic sight
Stirring this tranquillity
Routines of familiarity;
Taking flight,
Brilliant white,
Powerful rhythmic beat,
Extra-ordinary aerodynamic feat.
The flapping echoing,
Splayed feet skiing,
Huge wings skimming.
Worth the effort and pain
To lift and to gain
A new perspective and dimension
Head stretched out in anticipation
To circle and to soar
Then land on a distant shore
BEW '09

1. The challenges are:
-preserving the white (paint round the swan?)
-keeping dilute, pale colours for the shadows and textures on the swan
2. Experiment with dilute cobalt, or Payne's grey, or cerulean, or shadow colour on a scrap piece of paper
3. Try some pale dry brush for the shadow and form on right hand side
4. Decide on background: dark? Or water blue?

Art Continuers at West Street Baptist Church *The Way*

I am indebted to Lee Nicole Scott for her vivid image in correspondence[9] which expresses the process of writing as the 'untying' and 'sorting' of ideas and experience, before the compressing and distilling:

> "to untie knotted memories and sort them into colours and varying lengths and to create a bit of order in my busy head!"

Thirdly Creativity in Poetry

Watercolour painting employs technical skills of brush-strokes and colour on the paper, not mere copying. It embodies observation, imagination, problem solving, the research and exploration of ideas, artistic flair and interpretation. In a similar way, writing poetry is a craft, but an expressive and creative art. Like the painter, the poet can start out with an idea but the art form can almost take on a life of its own developing in new and unanticipated directions. I can finish with something new that I did not imagine at the start.

Human creative energies, imagination, and artistic works are, I believe, part of what it means to be created in the 'image of God'. Writing poetry is creative, not creating something out of nothing, but designing or expressing something new, fresh, impacting, something 'good'. The Bible itself is full of this creative energy, art forms in for example the design of the Tabernacle, the furnishing of the Temple, Hebrew poetry in the Psalms, narratives, the form of prophetic oracles, imagery, symbol, metaphor, and in the Parables and music of the sayings of Jesus, and in earliest creeds in the New Testament.[10]

---

[9] PRACTITIONER-RESEARCHER@JISCMAIL.AC.UK (accessed March 29th, 2012)

[10] After I had written this chapter a friend gave me a copy of Michael Cards' *Scribbling in the Sand* which eloquently explores the biblical foundations for Christian creativity. Card M. 2002. Leicester: IVP

The poem Image of God explores this understanding:

The Image of God

(**Hebrew**: צֶלֶם אֱלֹהִים; *tzelem **elohim**;* **Latin** as *Imago Dei*)

'Eikon'

'Eidolon'
Image
Likeness,   Character,
Form,   Appearance,
Visual or mental
Representation
In painting,
Or on a coin;
A semblance.
In God's image we were created.
The exact meaning is much debated.
Not so much in shape or form,
But in spiritual being seems more the norm.
A sentient, intelligent creative being
Capable of personal
Moral relationship,
Need for social and
Family fellowship.
God's representative
On this Earth;
Having dominion,
But protecting its worth.
The Creation and
Cultural mandates,
To do His will
As law dictates.

But the image
Was marred
Deformed, distorted
Through rebellion,
Not being conformed.
Relationships were
Disjointed,
Work corrupted,
Death came on us all
As a result of this Fall.
But through Redemption
Comes Restoration.
Where Israel fell short, Messiah came
Bearing God's image, The Second Adam,
A better covenant, and offering, a nobler name.
We now bear His image, of the heavenly man,
Being conformed to this image, is His plan:
Transformed into His likeness
Now by the Spirit's power,
Doing God's will
In this present 'hour'
On Earth, as it is
In Heaven.
Then in the twinkling
Of an eye at
The Resurrection,
New bodies for Creation's restoration.

In this poem, I am trying to express my thinking over two years or so about the 'Image of God'. I am drawing on the researching, questioning, and reflecting, then I distil, and compress in writing. I attempt to express ideas in a new form: the first stanza as a crown on a figure, and the second as a cross. I did not start out with this form, but it grew out of my interaction with the content and my imagination.

I find that poetry is not only creative in the sense of expressing ideas, painting word pictures with rich language, imagery, rhythm, poetic techniques in structures and forms. It is creative for me in its 'process' and discipline. Writing helps me to explore my experiences and feelings, and make sense of events. As I am writing, I am clarifying and expressing my ideas. This reflective process helps me articulate feelings, thoughts, values and beliefs. It allows ideas to bubble-up from deeper memory or consciousness. It draws upon experience, portrays, links thoughts, addresses questions, helps me develop understanding, expresses arguments, creates insights, theorises, and highlights truth as I see it.

In this next poem, there is a reaction to the earthquake in Japan and to crushing human suffering. I had been reading Peter Hicks,[11] and drew upon his study of the literature on evil and suffering and theodicy. Part of the creative writing process is the allusive dimension of poetry. It is not just the shallow thoughts of the writer, but the process draws upon references to other writers, to communities and traditions of human understanding, but avoids heavy scholarship, or esoteric language. I hope this poem communicates some of the 'shafts of light into darkness', to use Peter Hicks' metaphor:

Theodicy

Terror, chaos, evil in the news,
Earthquakes, suffering, revolution;
Crushing 'why's' that need solution;
Theodicy, theories, different views
Seek to explain and to justify
The actions of God, and answers 'Why
A good God who is all-powerful
Allows events that seem so awful?'
Is God 'Love'? Does He really care?
Of our human pain is He aware?

---

[11] 2006 *The Message of Evil and Suffering.* Nottingham: IVP

Some say His power is limited, or
That 'free-will' explains it more.
Evil allows us to develop and grow,
Or it's a part of the material world we know.
Some ask, "Does God really care
With so much injustice, life's unfair?
Why does He not act and intervene
To change the evils we have seen?"

Are there insights into this mystery,
A guiding hand behind our history,
Discerning discipline and judicial judgement
Behind the perplexing time-bound event;
Even the use of man's inhumanity
For higher purpose than the singularity?
God's name will be vindicated,
His justice revealed and stated.
At the very point of our perplexity
God enters our human history.
Suffering defeats evil, brings redemption,
Righteousness in the Restoration.
Perhaps it's inappropriate
To pose an impudent question
On issues, like Job, I shouldn't mention,
Matters to deep for my present state?

Fourthly, Poetry as Communication

Poetry not only captures experiences and ideas,
compresses thinking and is a doubly creative process,
but it also needs to communicate effectively. Some
poems may be personal, for the author's eyes only, but I
also want people to read my verse, to be amused,
delighted, helped, or provoked into thought.

On a teacher-researcher web discussion site,[12] that
was considering the issue of writing for publication I

---

[12] TEACHER-RESEARCHER@JISCMAIL.AC.UK
(accessed March 20th, 2012)

tried to sum-up and communicate my thoughts in a light-hearted way:

Audience is Everything

I feel sure that 'audience' is everything,
And 'genre' the next best thing.
A dense academic style
(References by the pile)
Is fine for the 'viva'
For the academy survivor.
But for an everyday read
For practitioners I plead:
'Write with clarity
With accessibility
For the profession.
During a writing session
Look to see who is 'peering'.
Write for those who are hearing.'

From Brian to amuse,
(Who reads and reviews
so many excellent papers
that folks on the floor
will simply ignore).

Even though this was written in a light-hearted way with educationalists in mind, writing for an audience is an important issue. I know an accomplished poet who writes in a dense, complex, profound style. When I questioned him about the esoteric phrasing, he replied that he writes for those who 'can' or 'will' understand. It may be necessary to be inducted into the language and ideas of some writers, or to wrestle with the thought until the initial bitterness of the grape is crushed with reflection or meditation before the sweet juices are released. So is audience everything?

It can be painful to have poems rejected or ignored by people. With some poems, I try to write with a possible audience in mind: perhaps for just myself, or anyone who cares to read; for groups of readers with particular interests; for individuals; or with a 'prophetic' edge speaking to any who will listen.

The next poem has had more positive responses than any other of my verses. Is it because readers identify with the ideas in their medical practice or in treatment received?

Some Nurses

Some nurses
Are real physicians,
Not just 'technicians'.
They minister healing,
Know how you're feeling.
They show warmth and empathy,
Express care and sympathy.
There is a kindness,
Understanding of patient distress.
They've dropped the protective mask
Of 'distance' while performing the task.

The gentle humour and human anxiety in 'CT Scan: Some Thoughts' have prompted appreciative comments from readers at our local hospital, on a poetry website, and in a survey:

CT Scan: Some Thoughts

Mmm… today a CT scan…
I've never been a fan
Of deadly x-rays,
Of revealing displays
Of the inner you.
It's radiation too…
They avoid contamination
Behind proper protection.
…and what will they find?
Will it bring peace of mind?
Can I have the operation?
What's the alternative situation?

...Well, I must manage my pain,
Use self-therapy this is plain:
"Is it true?" this introspection.
"Is it helpful?" cognitive suggestion.
Use some guided fantasy,
Self-hypnotherapy.
"Ah, we're really sorry Sir to tell you,
The power's down, no appointments too.
We know you've struggled through the snow,
Lost some income, but we'll let you know
When we can fit you in again.
We regret we've been such a pain.
Sorry we couldn't phone.
We'll do our best to atone."

Maybe these poems in 'The Hospital Collection' communicate firstly with medical communities giving a patient's perspective, and secondly with readers who faced similar experiences who can identify with the setting and mood?

Poetry as a means of communication has special qualities. It seems to have the so-called Heineken effect[13] with some people, reaching and refreshing parts that other forms of communication do not reach. Maybe it is something to do with poetry's obliqueness, its rhythm and musical quality, or its emotional attachment. Meaning can creep up on you, or suddenly burst in an inspirational way. The visual images, metaphor, or symbols may appeal to the emotional and visual centres of the mind, to particular or to multiple areas of the brain for fuller impact on the reader.[14]

---

[13] http://www.guardian.co.uk/politics/blog/2010/apr/20/nick-clegg-young-people-heineken
(accessed March 29th, 2011)

[14] (see Alistair Smith's 2002 The Brain's Behind It, Stafford: NEP Press). See also Angela Saunder's discussion http://www.bellaonline.com/articles/art9124.asp
accessed 29/3/2011... **continued**

As a means of communication poetry has a power often beyond the intention of the writer to amuse, to express, inform, give exposition, illuminate and give insight. As we read, we bring all our culture and human experience to the text. We interpret, getting alongside the poet's meaning, and we discourse together. We can get behind the text, seeking out the writer's intention and social setting, or stand in front of it… interpreting the text through our cultural lenses, letting the poem speak to us and responding in our own way. The reader may see things that are a surprise to the author. Of course, this is true of great literature, but in a lesser way it can be true of poetry more generally. I have had an e-mail from a correspondent in Australia asking what I meant in a poem, and the reader 'seeing' something quite different from my intention.

In times of self-doubt as a writer, I am encouraged that Christians who believe in the inspiration of the Bible also acknowledge that God chose to communicate through the Word, the Logos, and through the medium of poetry. Derek Kidner says:

> "The Old Testament repeatedly breaks out into poetry. Even its narratives are graced here and there with a couplet or a longer sequence of verse to make some memorable point… and its prophecies predominantly take this form. While The Psalms are the main body of poems in Scripture… they are themselves surrounded by poetry and rooted in a long and popular tradition"[15]

… *continued*
See 'This is Your Brain on Poetry' Ange Mlinko and Ian Gilchrist
http://www.poetryfoundation.org/journal/article.html?id=240250) accessed 29/3/2011
[15] Psalms 1-72 Derek Kidner 1973, Tyndale Commentaries. London: IVP

Fifthly, Poetry as Ways of Knowing

Poetry seems to involve a variety of forms of knowing.[16] It can be tacit, intuitive and an image-laden way of knowledge in which poetry articulates the awareness we have without our attention fixed on a subject. Tacit as Porter R. (2000) says is

> 'integral to the entirety of our consciousness, forming the background grid which makes focussed perceptions possible, intelligible and fruitful' [17]

Poetry can be the expression of an embodied consciousness.[18]

Poetry can claim to know through the senses, visualising, describing, portraying, conveying meaning as in 'Corfe at Dawn':

Corfe at Dawn

I woke up early that morning
To watch the golden light dawning
From Kingston heights looking down
Across the common to the sleeping town,
Wrapped in its misty early summer veil,
A striking scene with a historical tale.

Chilled, I gazed across the panorama
As the downs appeared in the cloudy drama.
Then the castle emerged quite eerily
From above the cloud mysteriously,
Resisting attempts to undermine
Glorious experience in a moment of time.

---

[16] see further discussion in *Poetry and Epistemology: Turning Points in the History of Poetic by* Hagenbuchle, Roland and Laura Skandera [editors] 1986. Hamden , Connecticut 06518 US: McBlain Books.
http://www.abaa.org/books/328344307.html
    accessed 30/3/2011)
[17] Porter R. 2000 *Tacit Knowledge in The New Fontana Dictionary of Modern Thought*. Ed. Bullock A. and Trombley S. 2000
[18] see Hagenbuchle, Roland and Laura Skandera op.cit above

Poetry can be propositional, arguing that something is so, or that this is the case, using reason to influence, or convince. 'River Out of Eden' was written in response to reading David Robinson's and Richard Dawkins' writing[19]:

River Out of Eden

Are we 'nothing but' survival machines
Robot vehicles blindly programmed
To preserve the selfish molecules known as genes?
Do we animals exist for their preservation?
Richard Dawkins has no reservation:
"We are nothing more than throw away
Survival machines. The world of the gene let me say
Is one of savage competition
Deceit and ruthless exploitation."

---

[19] *The Blind Watchmaker* 1988 London: Penguin. River Out of Eden 2001. London: Phoenix.
See also David Robertson's *The Dawkins Letters*. 2007. Fearn, Ross-shire: Christian Focus

Does this inexorably lead humanity to fall
Into the devil's doctrine, 'the weakest should go to
   the wall?
A polluted stream with the misdeeds of atheism
Rather than the so-called 'memes' of theism.
It's only one step from the swirling current of
   materialism
To the murky water of Hitler, Pol Pot, and Stalinism.
Thank God for Nietzsche's 'one great curse…
   intrinsic depravity'
Christ's example and teaching, and its universality!

It can be rational or evidential, perhaps arguing a case as in the next poem, which was a contribution to a web discussion on the CRIAN[20] Christian Research in Action Network website.

A Christian Scholar

You ask:
"Is there such a thing as a 'Christian' scholar?"
(Other than wearing a particular collar).
If a 'scholar' is a specialist in a branch of study
Erudite, distinguished academically,
Why add the tag 'Christian'?
Isn't that a 'private' faith, virtue, or vision?
How would a 'Christian' chemist
Be different from a Deist dentist,
Or, a medic, a Muslim urologist
From a haematologist who happens to be a Humanist?
Is it only the disciplines distinguishing?
(Faith from the public sphere extinguishing).
I'm at ease with a 'Christian' scholar of theology,
Rather than a theologian studying Christianity,
But is it the 'faith' that's critical,
Or a methodology that's analytical?

---

[20] http://transformingresearch.ning.com/.
(accessed 11th Nov. 2011)

Faith can motivate and inspire
The 'ground' of why we enquire.
What have we missed in discussions?
Isn't it the scholar's presuppositions
About the nature of reality, 'what's true',
'Meaning', 'a coherent worldview'?
It's not just 'Christian' attitudes or motivation.
Any scholar may arrive at my conclusion,
But the Christian has meaning, a teleology,
Of purpose, design in 'sphere sovereignty',
Rooted in Creation, Fall and Redemption.
We study within a framework of revelation,
With a Divine mandate to explore and explain
The natural, and the human domain.

Poetry can claim as in these next two poems, to 'know' from direct awareness or acquaintance, 'knowing as personal relationship'. These two men were significant influences in my late childhood and teens:

Fred Churchill

Outstanding to our generation,
Object of Sunday School veneration,
You captured my admiration
For exegesis and explanation.
I learned how to think and to question
Upsetting to some at the suggestion.

Your love for theological ideas
Was beyond that of your peers,
But their fear of the Lord
And your explaining The Word
Gave us a strong foundation
For Christian salvation.

The sadness at the parting
'One flesh' torn apart and smarting,
But think of the fruitful years
The love and joys now blurred by tears,

And the promise, "I go to prepare a place for you
And will return to raise you too."

In Memory of Jack Knights
An Old Campaigner

We've come to participate,
Give thanks and narrate
Your life, vitality and fruitfulness,
Musical voice, humour and playfulness.
'Chief': 'old boys' now salute you
For your dedicated service through
Our waywardness and youth.
You taught us Christian truth,
Gave us discipline and training,
Demonstrated Christian campaigning.
We caught the values and the vision
To fulfil your Lord's Commission.
Now beyond regrets, forgiven, at peace
You're in Paradise where suffering will cease.
Each of us has a memory to relate
To thank God today, and celebrate.

Images, metaphor, and portrayal have a particular place
in poetic knowing. I wrote this next poem after looking
at some old gnarled olive trees in Gland, Switzerland.
They became a metaphor, a symbolic understanding of
myself in a period of ill-health, which I transfigured,
with an enhanced insight into the everyday world, and
turned into a prayer:

LORD
As I'm getting older,
May my faith be that much bolder.
My prayer is I would like to be
Like that ancient olive tree,
Gnarled, misshapen with life's stress
But bursting with life none-the-less,
Blossoming and fruitful

For Your purposes useful
To bless others and to nourish,
So that our Faith may flourish.

Poets can claim not just to comprehend the World in their writing, but rather to be apprehended by an aspect of reality, that takes hold of them, or impresses their inward eye. Some poets claim to receive truth from outside themselves, a kind of revelation, or 'being taken over' in a rhapsody beyond themselves. Verse can express intuition, perception, inner light, glimmerings of the visionary, inspiration from beyond themselves. In terms more familiar to me, poems can portray the prophetic, or the illumination that comes within from outside ourselves by the Holy Spirit.

This next poem was written at a Vineyard chapel in Wool Dorset, UK when a lady leading worship brought a daisy into the service as a prophetic analogy. I have tried to capture what she said and how we responded.

The Ox-eye Daisy

LORD,
As the ox-eye daisy turned
Its face to the sun,
So we turned our hearts
To You Father, Spirit, Son.
I felt your acceptance peace and love
As we raised our praise above
The distresses of the day
Responding with our tears
To worship and to pray.

The next poem 'Shadows' shows 'knowing' through symbol, metaphor, analogy or parable. Everyday events can prompt a deeper spiritual insight or knowing:

We ambled with our grandchildren in the Autumn sun
Observing our long shadows walking and mimicking

That waved back, skipped, and hopped for fun,
Distorted and silent, yet speaking.
I felt the warmth on my back,
But the shadows were cold, dark
And spectral, projected on the track,
Reflections leaving a symbolic mark.
I wondered about the shadows I cast,
The effect of what I do and say,
Imprints I've left along the way,
The unintentional, hurts of the past.
Lord, I ask you will make me more aware.
To reflect your light is my prayer.

Poetry can express virtue or truth gained through the insights of saints, exemplars, sages, and Scripture. For the next poem I studied the words for 'forgiveness' in the original languages of The Bible, using the Scriptures as the source and authority for my 'knowing'.

Forgiveness

'Lifting',
'Carrying',
'Bearing',
'Graciously dealing',
'Sending away', 'loosing'.
God is merciful, gracious
Long suffering,
Abundant in goodness
And truth,
Mercy keeping
For thousands,
Iniquity forgiving,
Transgressions blotting,
Guilt and sin pardoning.
A sacrifice atoning
For the penitent confessing,
Wrath assuaging
At the mercy seat propitiating:
Jesus our ransom, redeeming,

His death substituting,
Representing and justifying,
To God reconciling.
The Father initiating,
The Son accomplishing,
The Spirit convicting,
Remission applying,
As we too are forgiving
Of those who are offending,
Against us who are sinning

"Oh the depth of the knowledge of the grace of our Lord"

Barry Percy-Smith and Clare Carney talk about 'knowing holistically and viscerally', and about possibilities for 'seeing differently' through art, but I think this can be applied to poetry too.

'Artistic media are particularly relevant to critical reflexivity because of the multiple interpretations and different ways of seeing that are engendered through representation or transformation of reality that takes place in the creative process'.[21]

Malcolm Guite discusses poetic ways of knowing at great depth. Of poets he questions, 'Are they offering imaginative insights, which are both internally consistent and consistent with our other ways of knowing?' He explores the power of poetry to 'renew vision by transfiguring the ordinary'. (Guite M. 2010)[22]

---

[21] Percy-Smith B. & Carney C. 2011. Using Art Installations as Action Research... Educational Action ResearchVol 19. No1 March 2011. Abingdon: Routledge. Taylor and Francis.
[22] (Guite M. 2010). *Faith, Hope and Poetry. Theology and the Poetic Imagination.* Cambridge: Ashgate. Girton College, Cambridge, UK

Makoto Fujimura[23] in describing his 'sitting under' Leonardo da Vinci's The Last Supper quotes Bruce Herman, 'If you want to understand something, you need to be willing to 'stand under it'. C.S. Lewis is quoted with approval:

> 'We sit down before the picture in order to have something done to us, not what we may do things with it. The first demand any work of art makes upon us is surrender. Look, Listen. Receive. Get yourself out of the way.'[24]

As with a painting, a poem may have a way of speaking, a way of apprehending the reader, rather than the reader comprehending and knowing. As we 'sit under' or listen to the poem, it can speak to us. We can 'know' in a fresh way. This is generating new knowledge for the reader.

Finally I want to explore **Poetry as Enquiry, as a Means of Research.**
Other writers will have explored this at much greater depth, as Rich Furman:

> 'In excavating his writings, Rich Furman (2004) explicitly makes the claim that poetry, including in this case autobiographical poetry, can plausibly be used as data for qualitative research. Furman is by no means the first to explore the relationship of poetry to research. For example, many physician-scholars and patient-poets have commented on the healing value of reading--and writing--poetry (Coulehan, 1991; Walker & Roffman, 1992), thereby implicitly suggesting such writing to be a kind of therapeutic treatment, the efficacy of which is presumably testable. More recently, empirical designs have

---

[23] Refractions. Makota Fujimura. 2009. Colorado Springs: NAVPRESS
[24] C.S.Lewis. An Experiment in Criticism. CUP. 1992

indeed investigated personal writing about trauma or illness as interventions and demonstrated significant improvement in outcomes of health and psychological well-being (Pennebaker & Seagal, 1999; Smyth, Stone, Hurewitz, & Kaell, 1999).[25]

This extract explains researching through poetry:

Learning, Teaching, and Researching through Poetry: A Shared Journey
Day, Liz[1]; Guiney Yallop, John J[2]

Abstract: This article describes how a nurse educator teaching in Great Britain facilitated the learning of her students when she used a poem written by a teacher educator from Canada whose research for his doctoral dissertation was a poetic inquiry. The writing of this article itself became a research project as the authors discovered, throughout the process, new understandings of what poetic inquiry is capable of. While considered new in some areas, poetic inquiry has a rich history. Monica Prendergast (2007) prepared an annotated bibliography of over 200 peer-reviewed studies that use forms of poetic inquiry. Both writers of this article have found that by trying to connect the past to the present through poetry, new understandings of self can develop that influence personal, professional, and academic perspectives. The cyber interviewer who poses many of the questions throughout this piece is borrowed, with gratitude, from Mary Gergen and Kip Jones (2008).[26]

---

[25] http://goliath.ecnext.com/coms2/gi_0199-21325/Can-poetry-be-data-Potential.html
(accessed 30/3/2011)
[26] http://search.informit.com.au/documentSummary;dn= 300407430428855;res=E-LIBRARY   (accessed 30/3/2011)
See also Furman R., Langer C.L., Davis C.S., Gallardo H.P. 2007

Poetry can be used to report research, but first, I want to illustrate poetry about research, that is, verse about doing research (in this case 'action-research'). The next series of poems speak 'about' doing research and action research.

Action Research

"Yes action research is a moral enterprise,
Not just a technique of problem-solving,
But about implementing actions that are wise,
With a vision of benefits that are life enhancing,
Improving conditions, bringing greater good.
The action researcher will be prompted to ask
Questions about 'ought', 'obligation', and 'should'.
This form of enquiry is an ethical task
To which we bring our values and commitment
That motivate and condition our researching
Its process, its end, and extent
For bringing 'shalom', real human flourishing".

Be Transformed by the Renewing of your Mind.

What perspective is there on action research
From practical theology or the Christian Church,
"Systematic reflection on a situation with a view
To plan and make desired improvements about what
  we 'ought' to do"?

Using 'ought' implies an obligation,
A vision of possibilities in a social situation
Through a spiral of technical investigation,
Practical or emancipatory planning and
  implementation.
We have a vision of Divine revelation
Through grand narratives and paradigms of Biblical
  inspiration,
And in aspects of reality, creational 'modes'
  discovered by investigation

The unfolding of God's decrees, Creation norms,
  and will,
Through Fall, history of redemption, eschatology yet
  to fulfil.

These motifs, paradigms we can bring
To critique and analyse any subject, any saying.
There are dynamic concepts of 'chesed' or 'shalom',
'Righteousness', 'justice', 'Thy kingdom come',
'Your will be done on Earth as it is in Heaven',
'Salvation', 'agape', 'God's rest', 'one day in seven'.
These ideas can illuminate our Christian practice.
In God's image we can 'rule, work, tend' and inform
  our praxis.
We bring any Spirit's gifting or Christ-like graces,
Ontological values to avoid methodological
  disgraces.
There's diligence required, humility, and love of
  truth,
Patience, 'fair comment', avoiding exaggeration of
  proof.

Such a vision demands we proceed with integrity in
  an ethical way:
'Golden' consideration of others in all we do and
  say,
So Jesus can be Lord over the way the researcher will
  live
As we bring glory to God 'taking thoughts captive'.

Christian Action Research

Is there such a thing, a concept,
Or is this a nature/grace confusion we can't accept?
Is there only 'a researcher who
Happens to be a Christian' too?
There are topics or issues of legitimate Christian
  concern,
Areas of life about which we seek to learn,
To make a difference by intervention

To change, or develop may be our intention.

But reflective practitioners will have a view
How things 'ought to be', what to renew;
Not just problem solving technically,
But a vision of the 'good life' morally;
Pre-suppositions about what is 'just';
A view of change that we can trust;
Assumptions about a 'view of man';
Beliefs with which to actualise our plan.

I bring my 'ontological values' too,
Embedded in, and motivating what I do:
'Image of God'; 'righteousness'; 'Shalom';
'Chesed'; 'metanoia'; 'Thy Kingdom come';
Transformation by my mind renewing
Making Jesus Lord of all my doing;
Critiquing action by 'Creation', 'Fall', 'Redemption',
Bringing all things into His subjection.

These poems were written for action-research audiences, or for seminars where I had introduced action-research.

However more importantly and perhaps controversially, I want now to describe how I believe writing poetry can be 'doing research', conducting enquiry, systematically reflecting about questions, issues or problems.

In short summary, when researching I start out with an interest, a focus, I want to investigate. Then I generate questions for which I want answers, perhaps more general at first, but then closer focussed, to probe. I propose and test explanatory hypotheses, and plan actions for change or improvement. Different disciplines have their own research methodology, but usually I have worked with a qualitative[27] methodology

---

[27] See e.g.
http://ejournals.library.ualberta.ca/index.php/IJQM/index
(accessed January 26th, 2013)

to improve aspects of professional practice as an educator.

I begin to collect data, information, about the area of enquiry, maybe from my own experience, from literature and journals, from observation, from official documents, interviews, and statistics. Then in seeking to answer my questions, to make sense of the information I have collected, I analyse, look for patterns, interpret, seek explanations, find key concepts and linkages. Explanatory hypotheses are tested, and action hypotheses implemented to improve the situation. I hope to develop new meanings so interact with the existing writing or wisdom on the topic. Hopefully new understandings, new practical wisdom, improved practice will result through my theorising, and perhaps other professionals may find insights in my written or spoken account that they can reflect about or implement thus developing not only my own but wider professional knowledge.[28]

I want to argue that in the thinking and the writing of poetry I often go through a similar cyclical process, parallel procedures of enquiry: data collection, iterative processes, interpretation, formulating possible solutions, or hypotheses, communicating practical wisdom.

Sometimes verse just cascades like a waterfall, or I wake up with a couplet on my mind. Other poems involve hard work researching the topic, by reading reference books, or contemporary accounts. There can be systematic theological or philosophical reflection and the distilling of experiences, and the finding patterns in years' of reflection. I seek to make sense of what I have assembled, and articulate interpretation, or clearer

---

[28] See e.g. the helpful explanations at
http://www2.warwick.ac.uk/fac/soc/sociology/staff/acade micstaff/chughes/hughesc_index/teachingresearchprocess/q ualitativemethods/ (accessed January 26th, 2013)

understanding for the writer. Then I try to make this all available in a compact and engaging way for readers.

I think in a limited way you can see the research process illustrated in the next two poems (both have received supportive critical feedback from poetry communities).

Earthquake in Haiti

A shaking
And quaking,
Buildings crumbling
And falling.
Chaos appalling.
Children dying
Crushed mothers calling;
Families destroying.

John Humphreys said, "Why?"
(A bishop tried to reply).
"If God is all powerful
Loving and merciful,
Why didn't He stop or prevent,
Rescue or circumvent
The terror of the quake
For Haitians' sake?"

We can blame the builders,
Politicians, town planners,
The West for insufficient aid,
Corruption, or warnings delayed.
But the 'Today' programme's question
The implicit suggestion,
And the Bishop's rambling reply
Still raises the issue, 'But why?'

There's a puzzling mystery:
Imperfection and entropy,
Suffering, decay, seismic disruption
Are all part of our present condition.
The whole of Creation

Cries out for redemption:
A New Heavens and Earth
The universal rebirth.

Haiti: The Cross Remained.

The cross remained.
The foundations not destroyed.
Yet all around crumbled,
The buildings tumbled,
Shaking and quaking,
The crushing, and choking;
The agony; the void.
Children bloodied
At their mother's breast.
Hundreds, maybe thousands,
All perished.
Hospitals were overwhelmed.
Society's infrastructure
A disruptive rupture.
In the Haitians' pains
The Cross remains.

Where was God
For this nation?
Did He just wind-up
Then step-back
From His Creation?
Was this a punishment
For the sins of
A previous generation?
What of the statement
"If you live on 'fault' lines
There are seismic
Consequences,
Not judgement for
Moral offences?"

At this mystery's heart
The Cross plays a part.

At the very nadir
Of our human condition,
God enters, identifying
With agony and pain.
Through Redemptive suffering.
Maybe we can't explain
The 'why's' that keep swarming.
They don't fly away,
But inspire our actions
For suffering today.

Even the next poem 'Day Bag' with its humour and gentle mischief illustrates aspects of a research process:

- assembling data;
- visualising, narrating and portraying direct 'knowing' through experience;
- perceptions; close personal observation and interpretation of the emotional pain of recovering from surgery for cancer;
- portraying the messy process of coming to terms with feelings about loss of bladder control; managing the medical procedures and equipment;
- narrating the process of coping and acceptance;
- developing a new understanding through writing and humour;
- communicating to the nursing staff and urology professionals in a way that may assist them in 'seeing' a patient's perspective, and maybe improving practice.

Encouragingly, the poem was received warmly by nurses at my local hospital, with appreciation by other medical staff, and I was asked if my 'Hospital Collection' of poems could be used for staff training in the hospital.

Day Bag

The well-meaning medical wag
Who designed this devilish bag
Has never tried to wear
This slippery affair.

You can't walk where you please
Without it sliding down your knees,
And with a catheter kink
You fill-up like a sink.
At the night-bag change
You need to stand out of range,
Or take a urinal shower
Of demonic power!
Don't expect the connectors to fit
They've confused the male/female bit!

So, poets can have aspects or dimensions of research in their work and make justifiable distinctive claims 'to know'.

I invited colleague researchers on the CARN[29] website to make posts on their understanding of 'poetry as research', but had few responses. However, more recently a paper appeared on 'Breakthroughs in Action Research Through Poetry' by Terry Barrett. Terry has outlined multiple applications of poetry in action-research.[30] In her work of facilitating staff development in higher education on problem-based learning, she describes the use of poetry as:

- a form and source of data,
- poems as an interpretive device on the issues of the poems' subject, and
- thirdly, the writing of poems as an iterative process, when authors find new meaning, and ways of communicating. She says, 'students used the poem as an enquiry into their beliefs... students were engaging in ideological critique by questioning their beliefs about teaching and learning... transformative action'

[29] (Collaborative Action Research Network) website (carn@jiscmail.ac.uk) (accessed Sept. 4th, 2012.)
[30] Educational Action Research Vol. 19. No 1 March 2011

'I view writing as an essential part of the enquiring action-research process. In my personal life I use poetry as a way of knowing.'

Patricia Levy also discusses poetry as research in a chapter in her 'Method Meets Art: Arts Based Practice'. (2009).

It seems to me that in writing, poets offer the data from life experience, go through a research process, formulate their interpretation, theorise and make claims, for readers to test and verify for themselves.

Here are some criteria, suggested questions about the 'claims to know' in poems:

- Is this poem appealing? Does it amuse? Is it striking, enjoyable, or does it inform?
- Does the text make sense?
- Is it internally coherent?
- Can I make connections between what is in the poem with the real world?
- Does it diagnose and adequately speak to the human condition?
- Does it have a 'ring of truth'?
- Does it graphically portray and vividly communicate its subject?
- Does the poem speak to them?

This is a development of Amy Orr-Ewing's questions in her chapters 'Isn't It All a Matter of Interpretation?', and 'Can We Know Anything About History?' in 'Why Trust The Bible?'(Orr-Ewing A.2011).

Poetry as a method and presentation of research has parallels with Narrative Enquiry.[31]

---

[31] (D. Jean Clandinin and F. Michael Connelly, *Narrative Inquiry: Experience and Story in Qualitative Research* (San Francisco: Jossey-Bass Publishers, 2000).

'Narrative Inquiry emerged as a discipline within the broader field of qualitative research. It is an approach to understanding/researching the way people make meaning of their lives as narratives'[32]

As I write in poetry there is a sense in which I am telling a story, and interpreting meaning. I am minded by Connelly and Clandinin[33] writing about Narrative Inquiry that in my poetry I should be concerned with

"the representation of experience, …integrity,… invitational quality in the text, its authenticity, adequacy and plausibility"

There are six criteria here to test rigour, and to evaluate claims 'to know' that can be applied to poetry I write, as a product of research.

I am indebted to Kaz Stuart talking about narratives (2012)[34] which I have applied to poetry: 'narratives are sense-making tools, and recounting narratives involves reconstructing experience'. Poems are representations of personal experiences, and can have empathetic validity as Dadds (2008)[35] has described, the potential of research in this case through poetry, to transform the emotional dispositions of the reader. The process of identifying and recounting through a poem can prompt reflection for the writer, and the reader. The reflective process of constructing a poem adds layers of meaning, and can create deep reflection where those involved can

---

[32] http://en.wikipedia.org/wiki/Narrative_inquiry. (accessed April 19th 2011).
[33] Connelly F.M. & Clandinin D.J. 1997 *Narrative Inquiry in Educational Research, Methodology, and Measurement*. Second Edition. Ed. Keeves J.R. 1997. Oxford: Elsevier Science Ltd.
[34] Narratives and activity theory as reflective tools in action research. Stuart K. 2012. Educational Action Research Vol 20, No. 3, September 2012, pp. 439-453. Abingdon: Taylor Francis.
[35] Dadds M. 2008. Empathetic validity in practitioner research. Educational Action Research 16, No 2: pp 279-90.

have time to reflect on and construct their own interpretations. The poem can be a sense-making tool, where experience can be reconstructed and new insights developed.

In conclusion, I have argued that I 'research' for and through poetry, to capture events, compress ideas, express impressions, portray, narrate and interpret experiences. As I communicate ideas, I hope my verse will 'speak' to some readers. I hope it will lead to changes in my own understandings, activity and practice as well as stimulate responses in the reader. This 'speaking', the relationship between poetry and prophecy is a theme I developed earlier in Chapter 3 Poetry and Prophecy.

This chapter has been a form of action research into my own writing. As I receive critical as well as supportive feedback I am learning more about poetry and how to improve my writing. While I have been composing this chapter I have been conscious of extending my reading and deepening my own understanding of poetry as a way of research, of 'knowing', and as an iterative process of enquiry.

I can see how I bring my own values into my writing, and how they underpin, or are foundational for my practice. They have become some of the criteria for evaluating my verse in addition to reader feed-back (some of which I quoted in earlier chapters).

In writing about values that informed my practice as an educator, I commented:

> "What has motivated me, has not been legislation or bonuses, but deeply held beliefs. For all my limitations and failings, they have been hammered out and tested through the fires of forty years of work in education. Briefly they have been 'Agape', 'Chesed' (mercy, loving-kindness), and 'Shalom' (peace, wholeness, human flourishing), and 'Image of God'."

I have expressed this as a pithy verse:

> "Of course justice is agape distributed.
> Chesed is the motivation for justice.
> Shalom is the fruit of justice.
> Image of God is the ground of justice"[36.]

On 7 Mar 2011 I wrote to Jack Whitehead expressing some of these values in a poem 'Loving-kindness'. I hope some readers may appreciate and identify with these words:

Loving-kindness

In a world of competition,
'My rights' and self-assertion,
There's much to be said
For the Hebrew "hesed":
Loving-kindness,
Mercy and goodness,
Faithfulness, solidarity,
Steadfast Love
Covenantally.
The energy flow....
Can you feel
The ancient wisdom
That we can know?

---

[36] E-mail to Jack Whitehead 11 Jan 2011

References

Barrett T. 2011 *Breakthroughs in Action Research Through Poetry* (Educational Action Research Vol 19 Number 1 2011).

Bertens H. 2008 *Literary Theory. The Basics.* London: Taylor and Francis

Card M. 2002 *Scribbling in the Sand.* Leicester: IVP

Carson D.A. 1996. *The Gagging of God.* Leicester: Apollos

Clandinin D.J. and Connelly F.M. 2000, *Narrative Inquiry: Experience and Story in Qualitative Research* (San Francisco: Jossey-Bass Publishers)

Collaborative Action Research Network Carn@jiscmail.ac.uk

Connelly F.M. & Clandinin D.J. 1997 *Narrative Inquiry in Educational Research, Methodology, and Measurement.* Second Edition. Ed. Keeves J.R. 1997. Oxford: Elsevier Science Ltd

CRIAN (Christian Research in Action) (http://transformingresearch.ning.com/).

Dadds M. 2008. *Empathetic validity in practitioner research.* Educational Action Research 16, No 2: pp 279-90.

Dawkins R. 1988. *The Blind Watchmaker* 1988 London: Penguin.

Dawkins R. 2001. *River Out of Eden* London: Phoenix.

Day, Liz; Guiney Yallop, John J. *Learning, Teaching, and Researching through Poetry: A Shared Journey*

Fujimuta M. 2009 Refractions. Colorado Springs. US: NAVPRESS

Furman R.: http://goliath.ecnext.com/coms2/gi_0199-21325/Can-poetry-be-data-Potential.html (accessed 30/3/2011)

Furman R.; Langer C.L.; Davis C.S.; Gallardo H.P. 2007. Expressive, research and reflective poetry as qualitative inquiry: a study of adolescent identity. Qualitative Research. August 2007 7: 301-315, SAGE.

Golden Bells Hymn Book 1970. London: Scripture Union

Guite M., 2010.
Faith, Hope and Poetry. Theology and the Poetic Imagination. Cambridge: Ashgate

Hagenbuchle, Roland and Laura Skandera [editors] 1986. *Poetry and Epistemology: Turning Points in the History of Poetic.* Hamden, Connecticut 06518 US: McBlain Books.
http://www.abaa.org/books/328344307.html accessed 30/3/2011

Hicks P. 2006 *The Message of Evil and Suffering.* Nottingham: IVP,

Hovdey J. http://www.drf.com/news/book-poetry-captures-essence-19th-century-hero-isaac-murphy (accessed March 29th, 2011)

http://www.poetryfoundation.org/journal/article.html?id=240250) (accessed 29/3/2011)

http://poetry.org/whatis.htm 'What is Poetry?' (accessed 29/3/2011)

http://allpoetry.com/

http://christianpoetry.org/

http://www.poetryfoundation.org/bio/ezra-pound.

http://search.informit.com.au/documentSummary;dn=300407430428855;res=E-LIBRARY (accessed 30/3/2011)

Kidner D. 1973, Psalms 1-72. Tyndale Commentaries. London: IVP)

Levy P. 2009. *Method Meets Art: Arts Based Practice*. New York: The Guilford Press.

Lewis C.S. 1992 *An Experiment in Criticism*. Cambridge: CUP.

Mlinkol A. and Gilchrist I. *'This is Your Brain on Poetry'*

Orr-Ewing A. 2011. *Why Trust The Bible?* Nottingham: IVP.

Percy-Smith B. & Carney C. 2011. *Using Art Installations as Action Research To Engage Children* … EAR. Vol 19 No1. Abingdon: UK. Routledge, Taylor& Francis Group

Porter R. 2000 Tacit Knowledge in *The New Fontana Dictionary of Modern Thought*. Ed. Bullock A. and Trombley S. 2000. London: Harper Collins.

Robertson D. 2007. *The Dawkins Letters*. 2007. Fearn, Ross-shire: Christian Focus

Sankey I.D.1958 *Sacred Songs and Solos*. London: Marshall, Morgan & Scott

Saunders A A. discussion on poetry and the brain. http://www.bellaonline.com/articles/art9124.asp (accessed 29/3/2011)

Smith A 2002 The Brain's Behind It, Stafford: NEP Press

TEACHER-RESEARCHER@JISCMAIL.AC.UK

Scott L.N. 2011 correspondence on PRACTITIONER-RESEARCHER@JISCMAIL.AC.UK

Stuart K. 2012, Narratives and activity theory as reflective tools in action research. Educational Action Research Vol 20, No. 3, September 2012

Wainwright J. 2004 *Poetry. The Basics*. London: Routledge

Williams C.K. 1998. *Poetry and Consciousness (Poets on Poetry)*. Univ. Michigan Press

Questions for Reflection:

1. In what ways is this chapter autobiographical?

2. How is it philosophical?

3. How does poetry 'capture' experience?

4. Give two examples of how the author distils and compresses experience.

5. The author says that poetry is a powerful form of communication. Which poem(s) have you appreciated most?

6. In what ways does the author claim 'to know' through poetry?

7. How is this chapter a form of action-research?

8. How can writing poetry be conceived as a form of research?

CHAPTER 8

DEVELOPING the USE of POETRY in the LIFE of the CHURCH

How sad to pass over poetics!
Insight is critical for exegetes
Of Psalms: rhythm of the Hebrew,
Emotion expressed, imagery in view;
Synonymous or antithetic,
The parallelism climatic;
The acrostic forms; the hymns of praise,
Prayers, lamentations of traumatic days;
Thanksgiving, penitence, meditation,
Dense construction, adoration,
Richness of language, exalting phrases.
There are questions the 'genre' raises:
Literary forms, getting into the text,
Gaining wisdom of the writer's context?
And even in the New Testament
Scholars perceive a poetic element
In Philippians 2 and in Colossians 1;
And even in the Gospel forms for some,
Of the words and teaching of our Lord,
Or in St. John's description of The Word.
Then, there's a rich, varying tradition
Of hymns and songs for the Church's mission.
We can learn our Christian theology
From sermons, and from our hymnology.
So here's an appeal, I hope not too terse
To include in our lives the value of verse.

The author wrote this light-hearted verse in response to a disappointing reaction from a reader about the value of poetry in Church life. He shares it here with appropriate amendments, as an introduction to the chapter.

This chapter will be of interest to readers who wish to think about the importance of poetry in the Christian Faith. The author makes an appeal for Christians to re-establish the status, importance and role of poetry in the contemporary church life where it has low esteem. An effective place to make a start would be in recognizing its importance in the Old and New Testament writings. A second step might be to acknowledge fully the role of poetry in the hymnology, praise and worship of past centuries. He argues that congregations follow their leaders, so ministers and pastors may need to review the example they are setting with regard to promoting the use of poetry in worship, ministry and Christian activity. Then a number of practical suggestions are made that readers might like to consider of ways of developing the status and role of poetic expression in corporate and private lives of Christians.

In the history of the Church, poetry has had a high status or significant role for some groups of Christians. There may be leaders who cannot see any special or significant place for poetry in the life of the Church. Indeed, there may be disinterest in poetry or personal reservations about its use. Reforming zeal to get back to the purity and simplicity of worship in the Early Church can overlook the role of poetic language or forms in the teaching of Jesus[1], the book of Acts[2], and the Epistles[3]. The Book of Revelation is full of examples of exalted

---

[1] This can be observed in the way the text is set-out in the Gospels in our English Bibles without scholarly detection of poetic forms

[2] See p.820-823, 886 for example in New International Version 2011. London. Biblica. (Acts chapters 1, 2, 4, and Philippians 2,6-11).

[3] See Philippians 2,6-11; 1 Tim.3,16; 2 Tim 2,11-13, Hebrews 5,9-10,12,13.

poetic language.[4] It is surprising just how much text in English translations is still set out in poetic forms and structures.

If this cumulative evidence fails to persuade about the high status of poetry in the Bible, if the reader is still unconvinced, then a reading of the book of Lamentations, and Song of Songs should tip the balance. Lamentations has striking literary features of a series of acrostics, and stanza forms. The Song of Songs is as Fee and Stuart explain,[5]

'a unique book… written in marvellous poetry, full of evocative and vivid images… a celebration of sexual love – and marital fidelity – between a woman and a man'.

Then there is the widespread use in the Bible of poetic language and techniques: metaphor, analogy, rhythm, imagery, symbol, and so on. This author asks the question: 'Why then, is there so much poetic language, forms, structures, imagery, and poetic devices in the sacred text?' We acknowledge the role and importance of different genres of literature in the Bible.[6] We have no reservations about story and narrative, proverb, oracle, psalm and song. So perhaps we need to renew our minds about the role, function, and importance of poetry.

The author is aware that many denominations or individual groups of Christians already recognize the importance of poetry in Scripture, in hymnology, in formal liturgy, and more open forms of worship. Poetic

---

[4] See the exalted poetic language of Revelation 1,7; 2,27; 4,8 &11; 5,9-10 & 12-14; 7,5-8; 7,15-17; 11,15-19; 12, 10-12; 15,3-4; 16, 5-7; 18,2-8; 19,1-8;

[5] *How to Read The Bible Book By Book*. Op.cit. See pp. 161-5.

[6] See e.g. the discussion in *How To Read the Bible Book By Book*, and *How the Read The Bible For All Its Worth*, both by Fee G.D. and Stuart D. 2002 and 2003. Grand Rapids, Michigan: Zondervan.

forms of language have purpose. The power of graphic language is recognized and utilized for impact on the mind, memory and emotions.

I want to argue that God allowed poetry a big part in his revelation in the Bible for a reason. It is true that poetic phrasing is a reflection of ancient culture, of oral tradition. However, poetry has a particular way of speaking and of emphasizing truth. It stirs the emotions, impacts the mind through vivid imagery. The music of the metre, and parallelism has an important role in transmission of truth making it easier for believers to remember what is said or taught. However, it has an oblique way of addressing the reader or listener. Truth can creep up in a dawning realisation, or it can impact the mind explosively.

The tools of poetry, the technical devices, are well known: rhythm, rhyme, analogy, imagery, assonance, simile, metaphor, onomatopoeia, metaphor, parallelism, parable, repetition, humour, irony and so on. The colour, music, pictures, and cadences of poetic language are contained in a space that calls for a pause, demanding attention and thoughtful reflection. Images can impress themselves on our mind. We can enter imaginatively into the poet's descriptions, and the meaning can burst upon the mind. After chewing over the words, or struggling with meaning the phrasing can explode with impact. Poetry has the power to move us deeply, to stir-up faith, and to lift our spirits to God.

In addition to the poetry in the Bible, there is the tradition of song and hymn. The poetry of the hymnology of the Western Church, and the praise and worship of generations can be traced back through history. In the churches the author has attended, we have had contemporary songs on digital slides[7]. We used

---

[7] Songs of Fellowship
http://kingswayshop.com/Groups/93622/Kingsway_co_uk

to sing scripture choruses, and used Sankey's *Sacred Songs and Solos*[8] in the 1960s. In our hymn books we can trace the rich verses of Francis Ridley Havergal,[9] the vigorous Methodist tradition and the poems of Charles Wesley in the Eighteenth Century, and the verses of Isaac Watts from the Seventeenth and Eighteenth Centuries. There is the earlier monastic music, translations of songs in Latin and Greek, right back to the Second Century Didache, and songs of the New Testament, and Hebrew Psalms.[10] The majority World churches have their songs, and hymns expressed in their mother tongue, and cultural and traditional forms of verse, chants and music.

In church liturgies of Roman Catholic, Anglican, Lutheran, and some Calvinist traditions poetic phrasing, collects and prayers are used.[11] The rhythm, repetition, and melodious phrasing are well known in the Anglican liturgy, prayers, collects, congregational responses and chanting.[12]

We have a rich tradition of poetry in the Churches in UK, and of religious poets[13] studied in schools and Higher Education in English Literature. The poetry of

/Kingswaysongs/Songs_of_Fellowship/Songs_of_Fellowshi p.aspx (accessed September 10th, 2012).

[8] *Sacred Songs and Solos*. Sankey I.D. 1958. London: Marshall, Morgan and Scott.

[9] *The Ministry of Song 1885*. London. J.Nisbet, and *Memorials of Frances Ridley Havergal*, by Havergal M.V.G. 1880. London: Nisbet J. & Co.

[10] *Hymns Ancient & Modern. New Standard*. 1988. Beccles: Hymns Ancient and Modern Ltd.

[11] See Gordon R.P. 1988. Liturgical Theology in *New Dictionary of Theology*. Ferguson S.B. & Wright D.F. 1988. Leicester: IVP. See his bibliography.

[12] See e.g. *The Alternative Service Book 1980*. Central Board of Finance of the Church of England. Cambridge: CUP.

[13] See the comprehensive article http://en.wikipedia.org/wiki/Christian_poetry (accessed July 26th, 2012)

Shakespeare, Donne, Herbert, Vaughan, and later Owen, and T.S. Elliot were all studied by the author's generation in school and college. It would be a great loss to the present and future generation of young people if Christians ignored or jettisoned this rich literary, human, and religious treasure. Similarly, readers will have a rich tradition in their own language, society and culture.

The author finds benefit in reading hymns, noting the metre and rhyming schemes, which can be models for our own writing.[14] Of course, we may have reservations about the content or theology, or wonder about the inspiration of the poet. Hymns and songs do not have the same authority of the Bible itself, and need to be evaluated in the light of Scripture. (Paul speaks of bringing all things into subjection to Christ.)

We can allow ourselves to be squeezed into the mould of society's dominant form of language: commercial or technical, scientific and rationalistic modes. Or, we can be subtlety encultured into one form or genre of preaching, or exposition, of a didactic rationalistic presentation leaving little room for the more creative poetic forms of expression. A study of the preaching, proclamation and teaching in the Bible, especially how Jesus preached, illustrates a variety of means of transmission.

The remainder of this chapter is invitational. I want to suggest how we might go about restoring the importance of poetry in the Church where readers believe it is necessary, where it has low priority in the lives of believers. Secondly, I lay out a number of practical suggestions for readers to consider of how we might increase its use in Christian communities. Of course, I am aware many societies and churches have a

---

[14] See e.g. Alan Gaunt's 'Always from Joy', 1997. London: Stainer & Bell. It is interesting to note the metric rhythm of Iambic, Trochaic, and Dactylic patterns of the hymns.

rich tradition of poetry built into their corporate life. They have much to teach us. One newly qualified pastor explained to this writer how much he had learned, and now employed in his own devotions and ministry from the traditions and liturgies of other believers. Perhaps there may be one or two ideas in this chapter that may also be useful to readers.

Churches may have higher priorities, but if we are convinced of the value and importance of the genre of poetry, it may be useful to review the role and importance of poetry in the life of the Church. We can ask the simple questions like:

- When is it used (on what occasions)?
- How is it used (in what manner)?
- And, why is verse is used (its purpose)?

We could look carefully at our range of activities, in for example:

o Formal structure of worship
o Praise, singing hymns, and songs
o Composition of new hymns and songs
o Prayer
o Preaching
o Evangelism
o Mission
o Festival
o Rites of Passage & ceremonies
o Social events
o Witness in society
o Defence of the Faith & Apologetics
o Teaching
o Meditation
o Personal devotions
o Individual ministry
o Prophetic utterances
o Home groups
o Work with children

- o Teenage groups
- o Other groups for e.g. ladies, men, senior citizens
- o Training
- o Family life
- o Personal communication

After carrying-out a review and establishing current practice, leaders can formulate and implement plans to restore the use of poetry in corporate life if it is deemed appropriate. When leaders know the place and frequency that poetry has in corporate and individual believers' lives, decisions can be made about how they would like to see this extended or developed. The important question is,

"What is appropriate for the vision you believe God has given for particular groups of believers?"

This may be the least of concerns exercising the minds of leaders with doctrinal issues, relationship problems, financial constraints and strategic objectives occupying agendas. Nevertheless, some aspect of the restoration of poetry in a church's life, or individual believer's experience may be relevant and apposite.

The chart below is offered as a tool for reviewing the use of poetic forms of language.

Area of Church life?	How is Poetry Used?

Area of Church life?	How is Poetry Used?

You may wish to skip the reviewing stage, and read on to the practical suggestions for enriching the language and creative expressions of meaning and truth. No doubt, the reader will think of creative ways members of the body of Christ can serve and contribute to the life of the Church by expressing ideas in poetry.

Churches could make more use of simple research methods such as feed-back cards, survey forms, and brief vox pops interviews to help the leaders keep an account of what is going on. One minister I read about recently[15] quoted feed-back he received on his preaching, and its impact. Another minister used brief interviews to explore sources of conflict in his church. He had strong motivation to find out more about a congregational issue. If leaders take the genre of poetry seriously, then they might see a review as one focus among the many priorities. A very useful resource for self-designed surveys with alternative answers, multiple choice, and free text options to questions is SurveyMonkey.[16] Readers could employ this surveying

---

[15] *The Dilemma of Preaching and Hearing God's Word.* pp. 22-27. Greenwood P. 2012 in *The Briefing.* 400. July, August 2012. Epsom: St Matthias Press. The Good Book Company.

[16] SurveyMonkey is free. It allows you to design your own questionnaire, with space for unfinished sentences or free text. http://www.surveymonkey.com/ (accessed July 28th, 2012)

instrument and analysis to find out the esteem people have for verse, and the extent of its use.

There are examples of Christian leaders enquiring, (doing research at a deep level into their service and mission), engaging in practical action-research to improve situations on the CRIAN website (Christian Research in Action)[17]

THIRTY SUGGESTIONS FOR REINFORCING THE IMPORTANCE AND EXTENDING THE USE OF POETRY IN CHURCH LIFE, AND AS INDIVIDUALS:

a). Ideas for Establishing the Biblical basis for the importance of Poetry

1. Why not make a study of the use of poetry in the Old and New Testaments? This could be an individual study, or a group or congregational study. If like the author you discover much about the type and nature of poetic expression, (the forms of language, imagery, structures, and use of metaphor, analogy and simile) you may feel more inclined to find further opportunities for using poetry in an appropriate way in worship, prayer, teaching, and service.

2. Reading, studying and singing the Psalms might be a fruitful place to start.[18]

b). Ideas for the leadership and life of the Church

3. What the minister, clergy, or elders do, or model, the people will copy. Leaders are models and exemplars so what they demonstrate in attitude,

---

[17] http://transformingresearch.ning.com/ (accessed July 28th, 2012)

[18] See the articles on the Psalms p.578-631 *Dictionary of the Old Testament. Wisdom, Poetry & Writings.* Ed. Longman 111 T. & Enns P. 2008: Nottingham: IVP.

esteem, and delight in poetic expression sets the example and influences the flock, and the cultural esteem for poetry. Human beings as social creatures look for expectations and models for behaviour.

4. Most congregations employ poetry in the forms of songs and hymns. But what about encouraging Christians to write, new songs, fresh hymns to express truth, to encourage faith, to comfort, and most importantly to express praise, worship and adoration to God? Why not set-up workshops for writing? Why not use newly written songs in worship services?

5. Ministers could use poetry more in services as part of worship. More pastors could quote poetry or hymns in their sermons. Why not allow the recitation of good quality verse in services? Build on oral tradition and memorization by writing and reciting about Christian beliefs.

6. Is there a place for more use of poetry with its powerful language in Christian festivals, in baptisms, funerals, and in special events?

7. The occasional poem of quality has more impact than over-indulgence or too frequent use of the genre. Perhaps reading and writing poetry could be included in ministerial and leadership training? Appropriate techniques and resources could be shared (types of verse; rhyming patterns; books of Christian verse; useful websites). To learn the craft, there is nothing like having a go at writing yourself.

8. Why not allow Spirit inspired poems to be read, or recited in worship services to encourage, comfort and challenge? (Ephesians 5,19. "Speak to one another with psalms, hymns, and spiritual songs")

9. Creative talents and gifts need nurturing, polishing and refining rather than suppressing or stifling. In the same way that other gifts such as music, teaching, preaching, flower arranging, stewarding, hospitality and so on are recognised, trained and harnessed in service, why not make room for the development of writing verse?

c). **Ideas for individual believer's lives**

10. Encourage the writing of epitaphs, 'in memorium' pieces, tributes to people.[19]

11. If there is a practice in your church of sending cards for encouragement, sympathy, prayer, or to stimulate faith, then motivate members to write words in verse.

12. As we discussed in an earlier chapter, writing poetry can be an effective means of meditation: on Scripture, on sermons preached, or on circumstances. Congregations need showing how to do this. See the chapter on Theological Reflection.

13. Expressing the meaning or interpretation of passages of Scripture, or Bible verses has also been illustrated earlier. Christians can be encouraged to take up their pencils and try this poetic meditation.

14. Writing prayer as blank verse has much merit, in articulating our deep desires to God. It is instructive to read the liturgies of other traditions to see how prayers have been written (the language, style and form).

15. Writing prayers out of the depths of experience, in loss, disappointment or pain can acknowledge

---

[19] This author has received warm appreciation for verse written capturing treasured memories of loved ones.

the real challenges of life, strive to make meaning, and avoid wasting our sorrows. We could encourage congregations to use the natural rhythms of their mother tongue and music or their culture.

16. Studying the Bible to find possible answers to those prayers can be helpful. Then using creative writing for possible replies (in the style of Michel Quoist[20]).

17. Poetry can be a means of expressing questions and admitting doubts. (As Jeremiah or Job). It is even more powerful if the writer wrestles with possible answers, or what God might say. By Searching the Scriptures and bringing faith to bear on issues, a Christian can write a concluding acclamation of faith, learning from the example of the Psalmist.

18. Expressing the main ideas of the preacher's sermon in verse form (not necessarily rhyming) can be a powerful form of meditation and internalizing of truth, as discussed earlier in this book.

19. A different idea is to take the name of an honoured or a departed person then to write an epitaph to their achievement or grace, perhaps using an acrostic of the letters of their name.

d). **Ideas for children, and for small groups**

20. Read the poetry of the Bible to our children. I was brought up with rhythm of one version that impacted my memory. The words, concepts and

---

[20] http://www.amazon.co.uk/s/?ie=UTF8&keywords=
michel+quoist&tag=mh0a9-21&index=stripbooks&hvadid=
21988794&ref=pd_sl_4ou5e0468p_e
(accessed July 26th, 2012)

thought forms have become part of my way of thinking. Poetry is part of our children's heritage.

21. Continue the practice of reading rhymes to children, traditional songs, the rhythm of tribal or cultural stories and oral tradition.

22. After a series of sermons or group studies on a topic, a person, or a book of the Bible, try summing-up what you have learned. Try laying-out the main ideas. Attempt to write in verse your reactions, or what you have learned. This could be shared in a home or other types of group.

23. Introduce psalm-writing to a youth group, leadership training, or home group. Psalm-singing in cultures with strong oral traditions might be relevant.

Read Psalm 147 together, or in a round. Start by writing verse one:

'Praise the Lord.
How good it is to sing praises to our God,
how pleasant and fitting to praise him!'

Then encourage the group to write their own responses. Model psalm/poems would be helpful to stimulate and guide writing. The meeting could conclude with the sharing of psalms in praise and worship. Psalms were originally designed to be recited or sung by the congregation. The next stage would be reading or chanting your psalms in church worship, or if you have musical gifts, singing the words. Chants would be particularly relevant for some cultures.

There are different forms and patterns of psalms: Psalm 142 is a prayer when in need. Psalm 136 is antiphonal where one person makes a statement then the group make a response. Psalm 119 is an acrostic. Take a word GRACE, or LOVING

KINDNESS. Then write the letters of the word down the page. Each letter can begin a new line, or appear in the line.

A well-known example of a single word acrostic:

> **G**od's
> **R**iches
> **A**t
> **C**hrist's
> **E**xpense

Try writing fuller phrases into each line. You might add a rhyming scheme. See an example later in the chapter.

24. An activity for a youth group would be to examine examples of hymns and songs on the Easter theme. Then encourage pairs to write their own songs. They can parody songs they know imitating style, rhythm, any rhyme and so on. They could use existing tunes, employ traditional music, or make a 'rap' where words are recited quickly and rhythmically with background music.

25. A productive creative activity for individuals or small groups is to look through the verses on cards for Christmas, Easter, or say Mother's Day, and see if you can come up with lines that are less twee or treacly, and have stronger Christian content.

e). **Ideas for Belief and Theology, and Social Issues**

26. A totally different idea this author has used, is to write poems about theodicy (the vindication of divine providence in view of the existence of evil). Take items in the news like a sudden death of a missionary's daughter, undeserved suffering, or natural disasters, and try to make sense of the situation.

27. Try posing a question about the faith asked by seekers, or by adversaries. Then write a reply, or a defence of faith. Attempt to write an apologetic.

28. This author finds encouragement and learning in researching the original words for key Bible concepts, then expressing them in verse. Try researching and writing about the rich ideas of 'Worship', of 'Forgiveness', of 'Hope', of 'have dominion'. Look up the names for God in the Old Testament, or terms for Jesus, then express your joy and renewed faith in a poem, or prayer in poetic language. This can be done privately, or shared in an appropriate group.

29. There are examples of using poetry as a means of theological reflection in the earlier chapter.

30. Creative writing commenting on human, social, or political issues from a Christian perspective can be a form of witness and ministry. This author has posted poems to web sites, on blogs, and discussion sites. Christians have an open door to use digital, web-based, and social media for Christian comment, witness, or evangelism. Poems can speak strongly into situations.

The more poetry is present in Church life, the more legitimate and natural it becomes in a community, and the less awkward or suspicious people feel. Try arranging competitions for writing verses: for new carols, as notes for a sermon, for special occasions. More emphasis on the expressive and creative forms of language brings balance to the more cerebral, rationalistic genres. Poetry too can be persuasive, polemic, and didactic, but it has the power to impact the emotions and provides space to hear in a different way. The truth can apprehend the reader. The reader will know what poetic language is culturally relevant to their situation.

Reviewing the use of poetry may be a low priority for the reader, and for their church community. The author understands this and does not want to overstate his case. It is not clear to whom the quote may be attributed, but there is wisdom in the saying:

"The main thing is to keep the main thing the main thing"[21]

There is so much to distract leaders from their central tasks. The author believes a priority for Christians is 2 Corinthians 5,9: "So we make it our goal to please him…" in thought and actions, and through the type and style of language we use to communicate. So, he invites readers to reflect about their own use of poetry and the way it can contribute to learning about God, to expressing love in private devotions, to public worship, to teaching, and to mission.

The purpose of poetry, the only thing that really counts is, as St Paul says, 'faith expressing itself through love' (Galatians 5,6).

---

[21] See http://thinkexist.com/quotation/the_main_thing_is_ to_keep_the_main_thing_the_main/219354.html (accessed July 31st, 2012), and http://www.americanthinker.com/2010/08/the_main_thing. html (accessed July 31st, 2012)

APPENDIX – Some tools and examples:

1. In writing your own Psalms in your mother tongue, try starting with:

    o   I will exalt you Oh Lord for you have……..……..
    o   Lord I take refuge in you from…………………..
    o   Oh Lord, how majestic is your name in all the Earth. You have……………...…………………….
    o   I will praise you Oh Lord, I will tell of your wonders of……....…………………………….…
    o   Lord why do you appear so far away, so……....…
    o   In the Lord I take refuge when…………………..
    o   Keep me safe Oh God when…………………….
    o   I will exalt you Oh Lord for you lifted me out of the depths when……………...…………………
    o   I will keep my tongue from sin, put a muzzle on my mouth from saying………………………….
    o   No doubt the reader can find more prompts from the book of Psalms

2. In writing your own prayers use simple speech, or you could follow the pattern of set prayers[22] e.g.

    Prayer for hearing God's Word used in the church the author attends:

    > 'Almighty God, we thank you for the gift of your holy word.
    > May it be a lantern to our feet,
    > A light to our paths,
    > And a strength to our lives.
    > In the name of your Son, Jesus Christ our Lord. AMEN'

---

[22]See examples http://www.churchofengland.org/prayer-worship/topical-prayers.aspx#diamondjubilee
 http://www.faithandworship.com/Prayers_Summer.htm
(both accessed July 31st, 2012.)

3. Acrostics provide a structure for summarising thoughts about a person. Here is an example of recollections of my own mother, one on the first letter of her first name Edith, and the second on her middle name Emily using the letter in the words.

Energetic homemaker

Devoted wife, loving mother

Innocent of evil ways

Teaching children on Sundays

Hospitable in so many ways

Your faithfuln**E**ss, and kindness,

　Your welco**M**ing smile,

　　Conf**I**ding, and encouraging,

　Reliabi**L**ity and spirituality,

　Sensitivit**Y,** generosity, and humility.

4. For further helpful and stimulating ideas and suggestions on acrostics see the resources at

   http://www.tracts.com/Acrostics4U.pdf
   (accessed July 31st, 2012)

5. If you wish to use rhyming words, resources for rhyming dictionaries can be found by using Google search engine, or at

   http://www.rhymingdictionary.co.uk/Rhyming_Dic tionaries--ll-4_634-Rhyming_Diction-0-0.htm
   (accessed July 31st, 2012). See also some free resources at:

   http://dir.yahoo.com/Reference/Dictionaries/Rhy ming_Dictionaries/?skw=Rhyming+dictionaries
   (accessed July 31st, 2012). This author finds a lot of help from the *New Oxford Rhyming Dictionary*.[23] When working with groups it may be helpful to have suggestions of rhyming words ready for them to use.

---

[23] Lennard J. 2012 Oxford: OUP.

6. For information for groups about different types of poetry try:
http://www.poetry-online.org/writing-poetry.htm (accessed 31st July 2012). Geoffrey Wainwright's *Poetry: The Basics*[24] is highly recommended. See also http://www.wikihow.com/Master-the-Basics-of-Poetry (accessed July 31st, 2012).

---

[24] Wainwright G. 2004. Abingdon: Routledge.

References

Fee G.D. & Stuart S. 2002. *How To Read the Bible Book By Book*. Grand Rapids, Michigan: Zondervan.

Fee G.D. & Stuart S. 2003. *How the Read The Bible For All Its Worth*. Grand Rapids: Zondervan.

Gaunt A. 1997 *Always from Joy*. London: Stainer & Bell

Gordon R.P. 1988. *Liturgical Theology in New Dictionary of Theology*. Ferguson S.B. & Wright D.F. 1988. Leicester: IVP.

Greenwood P. 2012. The Dilemma of Preaching and Hearing God's Word. pp. 22-27 in *The Briefing*. 400. July, August 2012. Epsom: St Matthias Press. The Good Book Company.

Havergal F.R. 1885. *The Ministry of Song*. London: J.Nisbet and Co.

Havergal M.V.G. 1880. *Memorials of Francis Ridley Havergal*. London: Nisbet J. & Co.

Holy Bible. New International Version 2011. London: Biblica.

http://en.wikipedia.org/wiki/Christian_poetry

http://www.surveymonkey.com/
(accessed July 28th, 2012)

http://www.tracts.com/Acrostics4U.pdf
(accessed July 31st, 2012)

http://www.rhymingdictionary.co.uk/Rhyming_Dictionaries--ll-4_634-Rhyming_Diction-0-0.htm
(accessed July 31st, 2012).

http://dir.yahoo.com/Reference/Dictionaries/
Rhyming_Dictionaries/?skw=Rhyming+dictionaries
(accessed July 31st, 2012).

http://www.poetry-online.org/writing-poetry.htm
(accessed 31st July 2012).

http://www.wikihow.com/Master-the-Basics-of-Poetry
(accessed July 31st, 2012)

http://transformingresearch.ning.com/
(accessed July 28th, 2012)

http://www.churchofengland.org/prayer-
worship/topical-prayers.aspx#diamondjubilee
(accessed July 31st, 2012)

http://www.faithandworship.com/Prayers_
Summer.htm   (accessed July 31st 2012)

http://thinkexist.com/quotation/the_main_thing_is_to
_keep_the_main_thing_the_main/219354.html
(accessed July 31st, 2012),

http://www.americanthinker.com/2010/08/
the_main_thing.html   (accessed July 31st, 2012)

http://www.amazon.co.uk/s/?ie=UTF8&keywords=mi
chel+quoist&tag=mh0a9-21&index=stripbooks&
hvadid=21988794&ref=pd_sl_4ou5e0468p_e
(accessed July 26th, 2012)

http://transformingresearch.ning.com/
(accessed July 28th, 2012)

Hymns Ancient & Modern. New Standard. 1988. Beccles:
Hymns Ancient and Modern Ltd.

Lennard J. 2012. *New Oxford Rhyming Dictionary*: Oxford.
OUP.

Longman 111 T. & Enns P, 2008. Eds. *Dictionary of the
Old Testament. Wisdom, Poetry & Writings*. Ed.
Nottingham: IVP.

Sankey I.D. 1958. *Sacred Songs and Solos*. London:
Marshall, Morgan and Scott.

The Alternative Service Book 1980. Central Board of Finance of the Church of England. Cambridge: CUP.

Wainwright G. 2004. *Poetry: The Basics.* Abingdon: Routledge

Questions for Reflection:

Little Brickhill, UK
Photo: The Author

1. What place does poetry have in the church that is most familiar to you?

2. What is the purpose of singing hymns and songs in your culture?

3. In what ways might poetry be restored in esteem and frequency of use in your home churches?

4. Which of the ideas suggested by the author appeal to you?

5. Which suggestions might be appropriate for the church you are connected with?

6. How persuasive do you find the author's arguments?

CHAPTER 9

METHODOLOGICAL REFLECTIONS

When I started out on the journey of writing this book, I was motivated by requests from members of the Art Continuers group (Dunstable, UK) to make available a more permanent collection of some of the poems I had shared with them. As I assembled the cards described in chapter One, I added a commentary explaining their purpose and use. I portrayed or narrated what takes place, and how we are employing Art and Poetry for mission in our activities. The chapter became a narrative of the work of the group in outreach and service to our local community.[1]

In telling stories about human lives, we reflect about experiences, select and organise the data, and interpret as we go, making meaning in telling the story. 'Narrative inquiry'[2] is the process of gathering information for the purpose of research through storytelling. The researcher then writes a narrative of the experience.[3] Connelly and Clandinin (1990)[4] explain that people are story-telling beings who, individually and collectively, live out the

---

[1] See the very helpful entry on this kind of research: 'ethnography'
http://www.answers.com/topic/research-methods-qualitative-and-ethnographic
(accessed August 31st, 2012)
[2] http://edr.sagepub.com/content/19/5/2.full.pdf+html
(accessed January 27th, 2013)
[3] See narrative inquiry http://writing.colostate.edu/guides/research/observe/com3a2.cfm
(accessed August 31st, 2012)
[4] Connelly, F. M., & Clandinin, D. J. (1990). *Stories of experience and narrative inquiry.* Educational Researcher, 19 (5), 2-14.

story of their lives. We listen to stories, and they seem to make a claim on us. We enter imaginatively into the experience of others through story, novel, and drama. It is with stories and within 'grand narratives' that we make sense and meaning of our lives (even though deconstructionists[5] and post-modernists[6] have made us more sceptical).

We build the repertoire of our experience and skills through direct experience, but also vicariously through stories. Professional competence is built on knowledge, understanding and skills. High performers draw on the 'rucksack', the 'reservoir', the 'digital memory' of direct and vicarious experience of cases, of stories. We draw intuitively on these past experiences in dealing with new situations. Through listening to stories we gain insight, come to see things differently, generalising naturalistically[7], from the case to our own setting and situation. Thus, the study of narrative is the study of the ways humans experience the world. People's lives consist of stories. As listeners or readers we have ways of appreciating and evaluating their worth. The narrative researcher needs to demonstrate truth-criteria, ways of evaluating the claims, or judging their validity.[8]

---

[5] See e.g. http://en.wikipedia.org/wiki/Deconstruction (accessed Sept. 1st, 2012)

[6] See e.g. http://www.allaboutphilosophy.org/post modernism.htm (accessed Sept. 1st, 2012).

[7] For a fuller explanation, see http://knowledge.sagepub.com /view/casestudy/n224.xml (accessed December 4th, 2012)

[8] Stories should not be 'hopelessly sloppy or subjective' as someone has commented, but be subject to criteria of reliability, apparentness, verisimilitude. As Connelly F.M. & Clandinin D.J. (1997) argue, they should have an invitational quality, be authentic, be adequate, and plausible. (Narrative Inquiry. Pp. 81-86. Ed Reeves J.P. 1997. Educational Research. Methodology and Measurement. International Handbook. Second Edition. Oxford: Elsevier Science Ltd).

Through telling the story of Art Continuers, I have been researching, interpreting, making meaning and reporting.[9] I hope that by reading this narrative and selection of poems some readers may gain some insight, be assisted in understanding or meaning-making in an area of their own lives. I hope some readers will be stimulated to take action.

In the process of writing, I began to articulate the theory behind our practice. In attempting to clarify our purposes and aims in mission, and our implicit values, I drew on an explanation we had used for an Art Exhibition at Priory House in Dunstable, UK. Through the thinking that writing demanded, I began to express my own philosophy of Art, a Christian perspective, that had developed over several years of reading, practice, and reflection. I focussed attention on our aims that guide what we do.

The chapter also shows how we have attempted to develop and improve how we run the Art sessions, and how we might make the morning more effective mission in communicating faith. The feedback forms mentioned in Chapter 1 gave insight into group members' perceptions about what they enjoyed most about Art Continuers and gave opportunity for suggestions for developments. I have consulted with members since several times about what they appreciate, and their criticisms. Chapter 1 in draft form was circulated around some people in the group, who confirmed it was a fair picture.

From this data, we have continued with the points raised as appreciation (the Christian atmosphere, the poems, the provision of ideas and colour reference sheets). We have also picked up suggestions such as

---

[9] For a fuller discussion of Narrative Inquiry, and rich source of references see *Personal Narratives and Policy: Never the Twain?* Griffiths M. and Macleod G. 2008, available CRIAN at http://transformingresearch.ning.com/forum/topics/truth-and-validity-and-policy (accessed September 4th, 2012)

running workshops of acrylics, and on flower painting. We introduced workshops on portraits, wet-into-wet skies, and painting animals. So, in a real sense action-research has been taking place:

- to improve the experience of group members,
- find ways of communicating the Christian Faith, and
- in the development of the author's understanding of Art, Poetry, and Mission.

At the end of each term, I review what we have been doing and reflect about how we could be more fruitful in terms of service, proclamation of the Faith, and Christian discipleship. The following term (we follow the school year), we introduce any new ideas or actions. (e.g. The cards and poems were introduced. The church leaders brought in a 'thought for the day' talk. We ran a series of seminars: Christianity Explored[10], Discipleship Explored[11], The Apostles' Creed study). The process of writing and reflection has motivated broader reading in the author about Art, about Christian perspectives on Art, and about poetry and Literary Theory.

The participant observation, survey, qualitative methodology, and narrative inquiry of Chapter 1 combines description, reflection, and analysis of our experience. There is a development of my theories on poetry and art, and on art and poetry as tools of evangelism. There have been action-research cycles of reflection, planning, action, reviewing and evaluating. In compiling this chapter, I was drawing on a range of disciplines and literature: Art, Poetry, Case Study Research, Narrative Inquiry, Practical Theology and Action Research.

---

[10] See http://www.christianityexplored.org/ (accessed October 4th, 2012)
[11] See http://www.thegoodbook.co.uk/outreach/christianity-explored/discipleship-explored (accessed October 4th, 2012)

REVIEW OF RESEARCH INVOLVED IN:

Chapter 1:   Art and Poetry

Methodology	Qualitative. Case Study Research. Narrative Inquiry. Ethnographic participant observation. Interactionist perspective. Document analysis. Survey feedback using unfinished sentences. Investigation of appropriate Literature references. Peer feedback. Pattern analysis. Action-research cycles.
Questions	What are the aims of Art Continuers? What takes place at the group? How can I make some poems more widely available? How is the poetry related to the Art? What is a Christian perspective on Art? How does Art Continuers seek to communicate the Christian Faith? What have other writers said about Art and Poetry that could inform our practice? What is the experience of the group members? How can we improve and develop what we are doing?
Data	Participant observation Verbal Feed-back from team members Systematic reflection. Survey cards. Verbal feedback from the group Concepts from wider reading
Analysis	Portrayal and selection of experiences Pattern analysis Key features of verbal feed-back Action planning

Hypotheses	There are valid Christian perspectives on Art. Art Continuers serves the local community by providing art activities in an atmosphere of acceptance, agape, and shalom. By reviewing the impact of the activities, we can evaluate the worthwhileness of the sessions, and the contribution of poetry to Christian understanding. We should continue to seek to communicate the Christian Faith effectively as part of the Church's mission
Outcomes	Dissemination of the author's poems Pre-evangelism, Christian proclamation and Faith-building. Being one link in a chain of events that have been involved in four known people becoming Christians. Development of a wider range of Art activities. Deeper understanding of Art, poetry and practical theology in the author Planning for developments
Issues	Ethics of consent and clearance. Problem of investigating the impact of Gospel witness and the activity of the Holy Spirit. A theological understanding of Art and of poetry.

I set out to do a content analysis of some three hundred of my poems to see the range and frequency of topics. There are poems about holidays, about the natural world, theological themes, some prayers, and poems about social questions and commentary, and about personal experiences. I collected them together in groups and one clear category that emerged was 'poetry and humour'. Within this category were sub-divisions such as of 'poems for children' to make them smile, poems about 'social issues expressing irony'.

Another major sub-category was what I called my 'Hospital Collection'. These poems explore and express the author's experiences and feelings during medical treatment. There are poems written as a kind of self-therapy, as a way of coping with anxiety and pain. They were a kind of cognitive therapy.[12] This collection received the most positive feedback in comments from two poetry websites, and a social media site CRIAN.[13] Medics (two doctors, five nurses and two physiotherapists) at the hospital where I am receiving treatment, gave positive appreciation[14], and a specialist cancer nurse practitioner asked if they could be used for training purposes.

Not all comments are appreciative. One comment on CRIAN expressed concern that a humorous poem was sexist. One poem 'Virtual Friends' received a strongly critical comment from a Writer's Forum poetry competition. After some appreciative comments and helpful points it said,

> "Overall this piece comes across as a rather sarcastic poke at on-line social networking, that doesn't really scratch the surface, and just doesn't seem enough to justify the writing of a poem"

Writers need to take the critique, weigh-up comments, and learn from the experience.

The author's research was autobiographical involving reflection and selection of experiences. There is a kind of theory building in the ideas expressed in the poems, and in the notion of writing as therapy. (The author has developed this further in a paper 'Poetry as process and

---

[12] For a fuller explanation see
http://www.rcpsych.ac.uk/expertadvice/treatments/cbt.aspx
(accessed December 4th, 2012)
[13] Christian Research in Action
http://transformingresearch.ning.com/
(accessed Sept. 1st, 2012).
[14] For appreciative inquiry see
http://appreciativeinquiry.case.edu/intro/whatisai.cfm
(accessed Sept. 1st, 2012)

product of research, and as therapy', delivered at OCMS Oxford Centre for Mission Studies, May 2013.)

Chapter 2:   Poetry and Humour

Methodology	Autobiographical. Self-ethnography. Interpretive narratives. Meaning-making through reflection. Finding Categories in the poems Feed-back from readers. Poetic Inquiry: using writing of poetry to explore and express experiences, to compress, and make sense, and to find ways of coping with fear, and medical treatment for cancer. Writing poetry as therapy.
Questions	What are some of the benefits, and possible harms in the use of humour? How is humour used in my poems? How is the writing of poetry therapeutic? How is humour used for impact in social comment?
Data	A selection of my poems Reflections in verse about personal experiences Items in local and national news Appreciative and critical feed-back Literature about humour, and literature search about poetry as therapy
Analysis	Extended reflection about life experiences Seeking patterns, groupings, key-features, and categories Interpretation and meaning-making. Applying therapeutic theories
Hypotheses	The reflection, interpretation and writing of poetry about traumatic experiences can be therapeutic 'Laughter is an effective medicine'.

Outcomes	Writing poetry helped the author to express emotions about cancer, and to come to terms with medical treatment more positively. Some poems have been helpful and encouraging to readers, some used in medical training courses. Reflection has clarified the author's theory about poetry as enquiry, and the benefits of writing as a therapy.
Issues	Getting access to the evidence of the impact poems have on readers. Finding literature on poetry as research, and the therapeutic use of poetry. Finding dissenting voices, and alternative perspectives.

I went through a period of self-doubt, wondering whether my writing was sufficiently valuable for publishing, or indeed worthwhile at all. When I circulate or publish on the Internet and if I receive little or no feedback, I begin to question, and to doubt the value of what I write. Over time, encouraging comments were made from family and friends, and in e-mails from the UK and abroad.

I wanted my poems to be gifts, a means of benefit, but heeded St. Paul's warning of evaluating myself soberly.[15] One motivation for writing was to bring pleasure to others, and another to be an encouragement or challenge in the Christian Faith. Some have a pedagogic purpose. I wanted my poetry to be a Christian ministry. I had had rebuffs from within the Christian community: lack of recognition of the importance of poetry generally; and of appreciation of my verse in particular. Then a close family member (whose opinions I value) suggested that perhaps some

---

[15] Romans 12,3-8. "…Do not think of yourself more highly than you ought…"

of my poems had a 'prophetic dimension', a way of speaking to people. Thus, this next chapter emerged as an enquiry into the nature of prophecy, and its relationship to poetry. I asked myself how my poetry might be prophetic in any sense, a means of 'speaking' to people.

Chapter 3. Poetry and Prophecy

Methodology	'Berean' methodology (they searched the Scriptures to see if these things were so). Rational discussion of alternative views, and of the author's perspective. Discussion of theological and experiential sources on prophecy. Illustrations of the author's poems that may have a prophetic edge. Exploration of the poetry in prophecy, and prophecy in poetry. Seeking evaluative feedback from readers.
Questions	What do we mean by 'prophecy' and a 'prophet' in common speech, and in Religious Studies? What was the nature of prophecy in the Old Testament? How are poetry and prophecy related? How is prophecy different in the New Testament? In what sense is prophecy available in churches today? In what ways is it legitimate to speak of poetry generally, and the author's writing in particular as having a prophetic dimension?
Data	The author's poems. Feed-back from Art Continuers, and a survey[16] Quotes from and references to theological literature on prophecy, and poetry. Contrary view points about prophecy, from my reading, and opinion in my local church Personal experience of worshiping in a variety of churches, with different views of prophecy in our own time.

---

[16] I made use of http://www.surveymonkey.com/ (accessed September 3rd, 2012)

Analysis	Conceptual analysis
	Exegesis, exposition, and hermeneutical discussion about prophecy
	Exploration of the categories of poetry in prophecy, and prophecy in poetry
	Illustrations of how my poems 'speak to people'.
Hypotheses	There is a close connection between prophecy and poetry in the Bible. Prophecy is frequently expressed in poetic forms, structure and language.
	Prophecy has not been withdrawn from the modern church as a spiritual gift.
	Poetry, and hymn writing can be prophetic in the senses of addressing listeners/readers with the re-revelation of the sacred text, and in the sense of Paul's writing about prophecy, 'speaks to men for their strengthening, encouragement and comfort', and 'conviction and revelation' 1 Corinthians 14,3 and 24-25
	Poems can have a prophetic element.
Outcomes	Clarification of the author's understanding of prophecy.
	Clarification of how his poems may have a prophetic dimension, and speak to readers.
	Possibility of readers clarifying their views of prophecy today.
	Draft paper circulated for comment.
Issues	Controversy about the nature of prophecy today.
	Discomfort, and reservations of some readers to my poems.
	The credibility of the author's poems in Christian communities.
	Danger of hubris, and making unjustifiable claims.
	There is an open-ended invitation to make responses about the possibility of 'prophecy' today, and of prophetic elements in the author's poems.

I felt a sense of caution about making claims that some of my poems might have a prophetic edge. This claim can sound arrogant, and be presumptuous. Writers need to avoid the unpleasant sound of hubris, or even mild immodesty. Certainly some readers have written to me saying that poems 'have spoken to them', 'brought encouragement', and have said 'just what I needed at this difficult time'. I hope that my writing may be a channel for God's Holy Spirit to work. An aspect of my action research is to enquire whether my poetry is encouraging to faith, and how I might develop the content, and wider dissemination to more readers.

If an author is reluctant to speak of the 'prophetic', perhaps some poems might lie in a tradition of wisdom? It was with some reservations about speaking of my poetry as prophecy that I began to explore the Wisdom literature of the Bible, and to develop further understanding of 'wisdom' in the Bible and to apply it to my poetry.

Chapter 5.   Poetry as Wisdom.

Methodology	Clarification of the concept and usage of the term 'wisdom'. Exegesis and exposition of biblical ideas of wisdom. Formulation of 'poetry as a Wisdom' construct. Practical Theology: writing more poems about faith issues.
Questions	What is wisdom? How can I gain a clearer understanding of wisdom in the Old and New Testaments? How do the author's poems reflect Biblical wisdom?
Data	A selection of the author's poems. Investigations on the nature of wisdom in everyday speech.

(Data)	Research into the meaning of wisdom in the Old and New Testaments. New poems by the author.
Analysis	Philosophical analysis of 'wisdom'. Analysis and exegesis of wisdom in the Bible. Analysis of a selection of the author's poems to see how they reflect the Biblical understanding of wisdom.
Hypotheses/ Pre-suppositions	The Wisdom Literature contains wisdom gained through natural revelation, by observing and reflecting about everyday life. It also contains direct revelation, as is the case for the whole Bible ('all Scripture is God-breathed') Poems can reflect both general and direct revelation. The wisdom of poems will be recognised by readers for whom it is relevant.
Outcomes	Clarification of the author's understanding of the concept of wisdom in general usage, and in the Bible. Justification for offering poems with elements of wisdom for readers to recognize and benefit. The writing of new poems.
Issues	The popular evangelical belief that all Proverbs, and other Wisdom literature are literally true without recognizing the social setting of the writing or the genre of literature. They say, 'How can the author's poems be wisdom, or contain wisdom? Poems are merely man's words, not The Word of God'. Are poems only wise when recognized as such, or do they contain latent wisdom for readers open to the spirit of truth?

Readers can reflect about the words of Proverbs, and apply them to situations today. The collected sayings of Ecclesiastes are like 'goads' to thought, and embedded 'nails' to help sound judgement. We are not expected to accept all the sayings as gospel truth, (e.g. 'everything is meaningless' Eccles.1.2, or, 1.18 "For with much wisdom comes much sorrow; the more knowledge, the more grief"; and "Man has no advantage over the animal" 3.18). By thinking, by meditating on the text, seeking its meaning and interpreting it for today's world, applying it to our lives, allowing the Spirit of God to address us, we are reflecting theologically.

In Chapter 4 'Poetry and Theological reflection', I study what we might mean by reflecting theologically, and then give examples of my poems as a process and product of such thinking.

Chapter 4. Poetry and Theological Reflection

Methodology	Use of Systematic and Practical Theological sources to clarify the term 'theological reflection' Exposition of author's poems. Clarification of the process of Theological reflection in examples of methods. Illustrations of reflecting theologically in the author's poems
Questions	What is theological reflection? How might one go about engaging in this reflection? How do my poems illustrate theological reflection as a process and a product?
Data	Selected poems References to literature on reflecting theologically

Analysis	Clarification of meaning of theological reflection Identifying the topics and processes in my poetry that illustrate 'reflecting theologically'.
Hypotheses	Poetry writing can be a process of theological reflection. It can be a product, an outcome of reflecting theologically. Some of the author's poems illustrate thinking that is practical theology. Readers might benefit by employing the methods illustrated in the chapter.
Outcomes	A theory that writing poetry can be a process and product of theological reflection. Examples of reflective tools that readers may employ.
Issues	Receptivity of readers. Acceptability to readers of the kinds of reflection described. Quality of the verse.

The chapter on theological reflection highlights a need for developing and improving the form, structure and language of my poems. In my study of literature at A level GCE in England, then in my training to be a teacher, I studied the structure and language of poets. Later in life I began to read more about poetry and literary theory. I was interested that some acquaintances were impatient with poetry, even dismissive. Some were not able to discern the author's intentions. A few correspondents could 'see' things in poems I had not intended. I asked myself why there was a variety of reactions. So, with the aims of developing the clarity of meaning and the quality of the verse I broadened my reading. I was engaging in action-research on my writing reviewing the structure and language. I wanted to improve my understanding, and the quality of my verse.

This next chapter The Anatomy of Poetry gave me the opportunity to examine the form, structure, and language of selected poems. I have narrated the circumstances that gave birth to the writing.

Chapter 6.   The Anatomy of Poetry

Methodology	Study of Poetics and Literary theory to illuminate my writing. Autobiographical narrative. Analysis of the process and products of my writing. Action Research.
Questions	How can I improve the quality of my writing? What are the literary forms, structures and language of these poems? How did they emerge, and what events stimulated the writing?
Data	Books and web sources on the theory of Poetics and Literary theory. Author's poems. Reader reactions.
Analysis	Action research cycles Application of theories of poetics and literature to my poems. Identification of patterns, structures and types of writing.
Hypotheses	The content of my poems is of greater importance than the technical structure. Concerns about structure can detract the inspiration of the poet. Ignoring form and structure can spoil the rhythm, and distract the reader's attention from the message. Poems need revisiting, revising, and polishing before circulation.

Outcomes	Making known the circumstances of writing, and the inner thinking of the writer. Development of the author's understanding of poetics and literary theory.
Issues	Debates in Modern Poetry about free verse, and ignoring the conventions of poetry. Controversy in Hermeneutics about meaning and interpretation. Evaluation of the worth and value of the structure and content of the poems.

This next chapter was originally written as a separate paper, where the author is feeling his own way to a personal theory of Poetic Enquiry. It occurred to him that there was a lot of research involved in writing some of his poems. The writing process itself involves selection and interpretation of that research. The writer draws on personal experience. It was not until later that he looked into Narrative Inquiry, and found other writers using poetry as a therapy,[17] and poetic inquiry as a paradigm of qualitative research.[18]

The chapter explores poetry as means of research, of expressing experience, and of a way of knowing.[19]

---

[17] See e.g. http://www.poetrytherapy.org/articles/pt.htm (accessed Sept. 3rd, 2012)

[18] See http://www.qualitative-research.net/index.php/fqs/article/view/413/897 (accessed Sept. 3rd, 2012).

[19] See e.g. the resources on Yahoo search:
http://uk.search.yahoo.com/ search?p=poetry as a way of knowing&fr=mcsaoff

Chapter 7.   Poetry as Research and a Way of Knowing

Methodology	Reflective thinking about the distinctiveness of poetry as a powerful means of communication, and a way of knowing. A discourse, feeling my way to an understanding of poetry as a process and product of research (not just research as a topic for poems, nor reporting research in a poetic style and form). Creative Poetic Inquiry is illustrated with my poems. Drawing on epistemological, and literary criticism insights.
Questions	How does poetry capture and compress experience? How is it a powerful form of communication? How have I used poetry as a topic of research? How is my poetry a process and product of research? In what way may we speak of poetry as a way of knowing?
Data	The author's experience and thinking compressed into poems. Web sources on philosophical thinking about poetry, and knowing through poetry. Literature on poetics, hermeneutics, epistemology, and qualitative research.
Analysis	Illustrations of the research process behind my poems. Analysis of the kinds of knowledge in my poems. Development of a personal theory of poetry as research and a way of knowing.
Hypotheses	Writing poetry can involve research (disciplined enquiry). Poetry can be a process of research: recording, analysing, and interpreting human experience. Poetry has a distinctive form of knowing.

Outcomes	Paper circulated on CARN, and CRIAN websites[20] Feed-back from peers, Personal theory of poetry as research, and a way of knowing. Paper on poetry as a process and product of research.
Issues	Need to explore poetic inquiry further. Dissemination of ideas. Invite a philosophical analysis of the paper.

In my studies and experiences about poetry and the Church I have contradictory evidence.

On the one hand, poetry is valued highly in Scripture, (particularly the Psalms, and Prophets). There is a rich tradition in the UK of hymnology, and inspirational poetic language in the liturgy of some churches. On the other hand, the author has encountered suspicion, and scepticism, reluctance to acknowledge the value of poetry. Perhaps it is because the Arts in general have been labelled 'worldly'? Perhaps we have inherited strands of ideas from Pietism or the Puritans in non-conformist attitudes to painting, drama and poetry? I wonder too whether church leaders expect poetry to conform to the pattern of the great poets taught when they were at school.

Different cultures demonstrate a variety of stances towards poetry.[21] Churches even in one town in the UK

---

[20] Op.cit earlier. Collaborative Action Research Network. Christian Research in Action Network.

[21] A web search on cultural attitudes to poetry illustrates a range of different kinds of poetry and attitudes in different cultures. Oral tradition in rhythmic forms has a high place in some cultures. See e.g. bibliography:
http://www.oraltradition.org/hrop/bibliography
(accessed October 4th, 2012)

can differ in their esteem for poetry. Whatever the causes or reasons, in the next chapter the author makes an appeal to restore the importance of poetry in the Church more widely. Perhaps the natural place to start for readers might be reflecting about the place and use of poetry in their own culture. Then perhaps they might review of how much poetic language and verse forms are present in their church life?

Chapter 8. Developing Poetry in the Church

Methodology	The author draws on historical material and insights. This chapter is more polemical arguing for a higher status for poetry. Practical suggestions are made to help improve the prestige and the frequency of use of poetry in churches.
Questions	To what extent is poetry present in the Biblical text? How is poetic expression employed in Churches? How might the important place of poetry be restored?
Data	The use of poetry by authors in the Bible. Historical evidence for hymnology in the UK. Invitation to review the use of poetry in churches.
Analysis	Illustration of the use of poetry in the Scriptures, and in hymnology. Invitation to review, analyse, and restore the use of poetry in church life.
Hypotheses	Poetry needs restoring in importance and frequency of use in some churches. Suggestions in the chapter may help restore the place of poetry in churches.

Outcomes	It is the hope of the author that readers may be persuaded by these arguments, and experiment in developing the use of poetry that is culturally and spiritually relevant.
Issues	"The thing is to keep the main thing, the main thing". Leaders need to discern whether any action-plan is right or appropriate.

Methodological Perspectives

There are some probing questions I am continuing to address about my methodology:

- How may the reader judge the value of these chapters? (I have circulated draft chapters to peers for comment, and revised parts in this light)
- How may they be reassured about the quality of my 'truthfulness' and truth telling, and the validity of interpretations?
- How might we judge the claims of the book?
- By what authority does the author make his claims, lay-out his hypotheses, and invite the reader to take part or experiment in 'Knowing Through Poetic Reflection'?
- How has the author guarded against unsupported assertions, bias or distortion?
- How do we know his arguments are valid, and interpretations justified?
- What have other writers said about similar topics, inquiries or issues?
- What is already known about the focus of these chapters? How does my enquiry relate to this?

In this diagram, I have laid out the criteria I have had in mind, which I have been applying to my writing, in description, analysis, interpretation and speculation. 'C' Factor communicates the idea of 'criteria' that have been guiding my inquiries and writing. The alliteration is deliberate as a poetic device to prompt my memory while thinking, composing and writing.

These are the criteria by which I would like my research and writing evaluated:

"C" FACTOR	Criteria by which the value, truthfulness, and truth-telling of these chapters may be judged or evaluated
COHERENCE	The principle of non-contradiction. Does the writing hang together, do points follow logically? Are there clear plans, intentions, and development of ideas, holding together as a whole? Is the writing internally consistent? Where there are conflicts, are these addressed? How are inconsistencies accounted for? Does the data speak? Does it support the points made? External coherence: Is the argument congruent with what else I know, and with what is already known by others? If not, why not?
CONGRUENCE	Is there a 'fit' between the points made and what is 'out there'? Does the data support claims? Are claims well evidenced? Are the claims or interpretations unbalanced, a-typical, partial or distorted? Would other fair-minded observers or interpreters say something similar? If not how does the writer account for this? Are the conclusions matching what has already been discovered or said? Is there an internal fit between the espoused values and values in practice? If not, why? What might be done to improve the situation to close the gaps between theory and practice, aims and activity, the espoused and practised?

CREDIBILITY	Does the writing make sense?
	Is it meaningful?
	Is it plausible? Does it 'stack-up'? Is it believable? What are the criteria for truth-claims?
	Is it well-supported?
	Are the points well made, even if readers disagree?
	Am I aware of the strengths and weakness of my writing?
CLARITY	Are the ideas clearly expressed, and well-illustrated?
	Is the language clear in meaning, accessible to the reader?
	Is the style and complexity appropriate for the audience?
	Is the typographical layout likely to appeal?
	Is there anything likely to discourage readers?
CAUTION	Has there been an ethical framework about respect for persons, rights, and privacy? Have access and dissemination been negotiated?
	I have exercised due care and honesty in handling evidence, avoiding exaggeration, 'spin', and deliberate or unintended distortion in interpretation.
	Have people been treated as an ends and not means?
	Am I treating organisations with respect and diplomacy?
	Am I modest in claims, avoiding pitfalls of political correctness, and seeing what I want to see? Have I avoided confusing what I should say (religious expectations) with what is the case? Have I distinguished between evangelical triumphalism and sober judgement?
	Am I reinforcing cultural myths or reporting truth as I see it?
	Do I have a hermeneutic of suspicion? In whose interest is the data given, or interpretations made?

(CAUTION)	I have sought alternative interpretations, and tried to justify comments. I have indicated weaknesses in my method and comment.
CONVINCING	I have tried to support the interpretations and comments with evidence and reasoning. I have grounded categories in the evidence when appropriate. Drafts of chapters have been circulated to peers for critical feedback. Comments and suggestions have been taken seriously, and the text revised. Are the arguments believable? Readers will be the judge. I have tested them on friends and academic peers. I have assembled arguments, support from other writers, and marshalled data to be persuasive.
COMPREHENSIVE	The book is certainly comprehensive in the sense of 'a large content or scope; wide ranging'.[22] Is it comprehensive in the sense of dealing with all or many aspects of something? Chapters include a range of views, and contrary ideas are discussed. There is the possibility of distortion in respondents trying to please, or leaving unspoken negative comments. The author has attempted to be comprehensive in terms of the explanatory power of the theories he has developed. More could have been included on prophetic writing of other authors. Chapters were made more comprehensive in the light of peer review.

[22] *Concise Oxford English Dictionary* p.293. Ed. Pearsall J. 2002. Oxford: OUP.

CREATIVITY	The author has been creatively involved in employing Art in mission for seven years. He has tried linking poetry with Art to communicate, and impact readers. Narrative Inquiry and particularly Poetic Inquiry are creative forms of research. The process of the research method and its outcomes are Arts-based. When the author commenced the book, he found very little on poetry as way of knowing, and a process of research. The journey has been creative, and innovatory.
CITATIONS	"By what authority do you do and say these things?" There are extensive references to appropriate literature, and citations from authors. I have made use of footnotes to improve the readability by avoiding distracting references in the text itself. Evidence is cited to support points made. Extensive reference has been made to Internet sources.
CREDENTIALS	The author has written over three hundred poems, some of which have been published on the Web and elsewhere. Much of the writing is based on life experience. He is an experienced action-researcher, and a mentor for research at OCMS Oxford. He has a publishing record in education. He is a genuine 'enquirer', seeking to develop, and make more effective his service as a Christian. He is ultimately accountable to God.
'CHARIS'	The author has tried to be fair to perspectives with which he disagrees, to be charitable, and gracious to other points of view. He hopes any gifting he shows will be appreciated and of benefit to others.

('CHARIS')	He invites responses from readers that will be received in the same spirit.
	At the end of all this research and writing there is the question of "So, what?" This is an important question. What difference has all this made to
	-my own understandings?
	-to my practice as a Christian worker?
	-to adding to knowledge about mission, practical theology, poetic inquiry, the availability of the author's poems, and to research methodology?
	I have attempted to answer these questions in the text.

I hope it has become clear to the reader as each chapter has been read, or as you have browsed, or picked parts of interest, that the writing of this book has been the means of developing my understanding across a range of subjects: Art, Mission, Poetics, and Practical Theology.

This study has helped me develop my theories of:

-   'Christian' Art
-   Poetry as prophecy
-   Poetry as wisdom
-   How writing verse aids theological reflection
-   How detailed research can be involved in composing verse
-   How we can claim that poetry is a process of research
-   How we can claim to 'know' in our poetry

This thinking, experiment, and writing has contributed to my service as a Christian by:

-   Reviewing, evaluating and planning to improve Art Continuers, to make it a better experience for group members, and to take action in communicating our Faith. This was research to inform action.

- Reflection about my writing of poetry has informed me about structure, rhythms, and poetic language. It has renewed my desire to write verse that is informative, helpful and faith-building. I am encouraged to continue writing.
- It has reinforced my efforts to disseminate my poems more widely.
- I pray they may be used by the Holy Spirit to 'strengthen, encourage and comfort' believers, and to communicate the Faith in mission, evangelism and apologetics.

I believe the book has added to current literature a new description of using Art and Poetry in mission. Chapter 1 is an original account of evangelism, proclamation and demonstration of the Christian Faith employing Art. The chapters on poetry and prophecy, and poetry and wisdom contribute new insights to Practical Theology. My investigation into poetry as a form of knowing, and a way of researching contributes to the literature on Poetic Inquiry.

References

CARN (Collaborative Action Research Network)
http://www.esri.mmu.ac.uk/carnnew/

Connelly F.M. & Clandinin D.J. (1997) Narrative
Inquiry. Pp. 81-86. Ed Reeves J.P. 1997. *Educational
Research. Methodology and Measurement. International
Handbook*. Second Edition. Oxford: Elsevier Science
Ltd.

Connelly, F. M., & Clandinin, D. J. (1990). Stories of
experience and narrative inquiry. Educational
Researcher, 19 (5), 2-14.

Concise Oxford English Dictionary p.293. Ed. Pearsall J.
2002. Oxford: OUP.

CRIAN (Christian Action Research Network)
http://transformingresearch.ning.com/
(accessed Sept. 4th 2012)

Griffiths M. and Macleod G. 2008, available CRIAN at
http://transformingresearch.ning.com/forum/topics
/truth-and-validity-and-policy
(accessed September 4th, 2012)

Holy Bible. NIV.1992, Cambridge: CUP.

http://uk.search.yahoo.com/search?p=poetry as a way
of knowing&fr=mcsaoff

http://www.allaboutphilosophy.org/postmodernism.
htm (accessed Sept. 1st, 2012)

http://www.answers.com/topic/research-methods-
qualitative-and-ethnographic
(accessed August 31st, 2012)

http://appreciativeinquiry.case.edu/intro/whatisai.cfm
(accessed Sept. 1st, 2012)

http://www.poetrytherapy.org/articles/pt.htm
(accessed Sept. 3rd, 2012)

http://www.qualitative-
research.net/index.php/fqs/article/view/413/897
(accessed Sept. 3rd, 2012).

http://www.surveymonkey.com/
(accessed September 3rd, 2012)

http://en.wikipedia.org/wiki/Deconstruction
(accessed Sept. 1st, 2012)

http://writing.colostate.edu/guides/research/observe/c
om3a2.cfm
(accessed August 31st, 2012)

http://writing.colostate.edu/guides/research/casestudy
/com2a1.cfm
(accessed August 31st, 2012)

Questions for Reflection:

---

1. How did the author use poetry and art for mission?

2. How can story telling be a method and product of research?

3. What truth criteria might we use to judge the research value of narrative?

4. What were the outcomes of Chapter 2, Poetry and Humour?

5. What background research was necessary for Chapter 3, Poetry and Prophecy?

6. How was the research process different in Chapter 4 from Chapter 1?

7. What are two methods of theological reflection described in Chapter 4?

8. What were the research questions in Chapter 6, The Anatomy of Poetry?

9. Did the author's hypotheses emerge in for example, Chapter 7, before or during the writing?

10. What would you say are three strengths and two weaknesses in the author's methodology?